Third Edition

STUDYING RHYTHM

ANNE CAROTHERS HALL
Wilfrid Laurier University

PEARSON
Prentice Hall

Upper Saddle River, New Jersey 07458

This book is dedicated
to the memory of Wallace Berry

Editor-in-Chief: Sarah Touborg
Senior Acquisitions Editor: Christopher T. Johnson
Editorial Assistant: Evette Dickerson
Marketing Manager: Sheryl Adams
Marketing Assistant: Cherron Gardner
Managing Editor: Joanne Riker
Production Editor: Laura A. Lawrie
Manufacturing and Prepress Buyer: Benjamin D. Smith
Cover Designer: Bruce Kenselaar
Composition: This book was set in 10/12 Times by Stratford Publishing Services
Printer/Binder: Interior printed by Courier Companies. The cover was printed by Phoenix Color Corp.

Credits and acknowledgments borrowed from other sources and reproduced, with permission, in this textbook appear on appropriate page within text.

Pearson Education LTD.
Pearson Education Singapore, Pte. Ltd
Pearson Education, Canada, Ltd
Pearson Education-Japan

Pearson Education Australia PTY, Limited
Pearson Education North Asia Ltd
Pearson Educación de Mexico, S.A. de C.V.
Pearson Education Malaysia, Pte/Ltd

10 9 8
ISBN 0-13-040602-3

CONTENTS

INTRODUCTION

This book contains extended rhythmic studies and preparatory exercises. They are intended to help students learn to perform the rhythmic patterns most frequently encountered in Western art music. Familiarity with rhythmic patterns, along with a habit of understanding rhythm in phrase-length structures, should facilitate actual musical performance, in which we must be concerned with all the parameters of music. The modest aim of this book explains why there are no studies involving pitch.

The exercises and studies are meant to be sung; in two- and three-part studies, the additional lines may be tapped or clapped. Singing is best because, unlike speaking, it promotes the conviction that we are engaged in a musical activity, and, unlike clapping, it allows us to give the notes their full durations, rather than to perform only the pattern of attacks.

The exercises, identified by numbers following the chapter number (1.1, 3.2), serve as preparation for the studies that follow them. Most of them consist of single measures, or pairs of measures, separated by whole-measure rests. Metronome markings for an exercise suggest a range of tempi possible for the performance of all its segments, but individual segments may be performed faster. Each segment of an exercise should be repeated several times, until it is easy, before we proceed to the next segment. The ability to repeat a pattern is evidence that we can perform it; unless we can perform a pattern three or four times in succession, we have not conquered it. Spending enough time on a segment to memorize it is a good way to ensure that the rhythmic pattern has been completely grasped. These patterns are the equivalent of words in a rhythmic vocabulary, and we should be able to perform them without thinking about the individual values, just as we can read a word we know and not have to think how each letter is pronounced. The exercises do not necessarily offer complete preparation for the following studies; rather, they serve as models. Where individual patterns in the studies seem difficult, they should be extracted and practiced.

The studies are identified by letters following the chapter number (1.A, 3.B). They are composed of well-defined phrases grouped in such simple musical forms as statement, contrast, and return, or statement and variations. Just as a verbal phrase is a group of words that belong together because they make sense as a unit within a larger structure, a musical phrase is a group of notes that belong together because they make musical sense as a unit within a larger structure. The most practical definition of a musical phrase is "a group of notes that we would want to sing on one breath." In fact, that is the way a phrase should be sung—on one breath, with the beginning and end usually defined by silence. For the most part the phrases in the studies are not marked, but are visible because they are separated by rests. Occasionally only a comma indicates where the performer must sneak a breath without significantly delaying the beat. Where rests within phrases make the phrasing ambiguous, phrase marks are given.

In performing the studies, the goal must always be to grasp the rhythm of the phrase as a whole. Reading music note-by-note is as useless as reading prose letter-by-letter. Reading a beat at a time is like reading a word at a time, and the lack of comprehension will be audible whether the performer is reading music or poetry. A musical phrase, a musical gesture, must be comprehended as a whole. To break a phrase, by hesitating or by repeating a fragment, is to destroy it. We must arrive at cadences on time; in ensemble performance, arriving late is embarrassing, to say the least. So while we should aim for absolute accuracy, we miss the point if we concentrate on the details at the expense of the shape of the long phrase. The phrase must be understood as a continuous flow, articulated and enlivened by the patterns within it.

If sustaining the phrase is important, so is breathing between phrases. An unbroken flow of sound, like too many run-on sentences, makes both performer and listener physically uncomfortable—out of breath. Breathing is vital.

The last study in each chapter is a rhythmic setting of a short poem, or a fragment of a poem or piece of prose, that has something to do with music. While the texts are intended to make the book more interesting, the fit between the natural spoken verbal rhythm and the musical rhythm should make it easier for the performer to become comfortable with some of the rhythmic patterns. For example,

may seem simpler and more natural when it is the setting of the beginning of the Hopkins poem:

$$\frac{2}{4}\ \flat\ \downarrow\quad \boxed{}\ |\ \boxed{}\ \downarrow\quad \flat\ |\ \downarrow$$

Noth-ing   is so beau-ti-ful   as Spring

The text-settings are given dynamic markings, as are some of the other studies in the book. Keeping the tempo steady through changes in dynamics is a basic performance skill. As, in a sense, *loud* and *slow* both mean *big,* it may help us keep the tempo steady if we think *loud* means *slow.* The absence of dynamic markings in any given study does not mean that it should be performed mezzo forte or with the same dynamic level from beginning to end. When only the rhythm and tempo are given, performers are encouraged to exercise imagination in varying dynamics within and between studies in ways that suit the rhythm. Phrases and whole studies may be clarified and shaped and given direction through changes of dynamics. Where patterns or phrases are repeated, the repetition can be softer, as an echo, or louder, for increased emphasis. Lightness facilitates speed, and so whole studies may be performed pianissimo, especially where the rhythm is quick and complicated, to combat the unhelpful tendency to reflect the stress of performing something difficult by making it louder.

That no pitch is notated does not mean that we must sing all the notes on the same pitch. Making up tunes to fit the rhythmic patterns and mood can be both entertaining and instructive. The tune may be as simple as going up and down a scale, changing direction so that rhythmically important points are high points in the melodic line. In group performance, as in class, different singers can be assigned different notes of a triad, or even different voices in a harmonic progression.

There may be no better way to achieve the familiarity with a rhythmic pattern that makes us feel we own it than to compose a phrase or two that incorporates the pattern. Finding a text that can reasonably be set using a given rhythmic pattern can be both challenging and fun. The texts set in this book suggest some sources, as they are often parts of poems of which other parts could well be set with similar rhythms, and other poems by the same poet may offer similar possibilities.

In notating rhythms, we should strive to make the spacing of the notes reflect their relative durations. In writing ♩. ♩ ♩, for example, almost three times as much space must be left after the dotted eighth as after the sixteenth. Notes must also be beamed correctly to show beats. Accuracy in notation is necessary if anyone else is to read it, and, just as important, it sensitizes us to the assistance proper notation gives us in reading rhythm: ¾ ♩ ♪ ♫ ♫ is much more difficult to read than the same pattern written with correct spacing and beams: ¾ ♩ ♩ ♩ ♫.

The two-part and three-part studies may be performed with one or more people on each part, but they are designed for solo performance. In the two-part studies, the upper part should be sung and the lower part tapped or clapped. Although it may be easier to tap both parts, singing one part and tapping the other is a better way to learn to hear two independent parts rather than just one composite pattern. The three-part studies should be performed with voice and two hands, or with voice, hand, and foot. Most musicians will find these two- and three-part studies much more difficult than the single lines. However, as so much of our music is composed of several lines, each with its own integrity, developing the ability to think two and even three rhythms at once is well worth the effort.

In all the exercises and studies, notes in the sung parts must be given their full durations (except when we snatch a breath between phrases). Accurate performance does not allow us to begin a silence too soon, or to add a silence, any more than it allows us to begin a sound too soon, or to add a sound. Because we tend to concentrate on beginning each note at the right time, we often find it difficult to listen to the full duration of each sound, to pay attention to its continuation and ending. However, in order to project a line, we must hear the whole of every sound. Again, this is why singing the studies is better than clapping them.

In spite of this recommendation to sing the rhythms, clapping and counting aloud may be a good way to begin learning them. We do have to be able to count beats. When the beats are divided and subdivided, we may want to begin by articulating all the smallest divisions, so as to be sure to get the proportions of the values correct:

While we must strive for the accurate performance this facilitates, we must also work to hear patterns of notes of different durations within a beat: an eighth-note may take the time of two sixteenth-notes, but it is not two sixteenths added together, so eventually we must be able to count just the beats and hear the patterns within them. Aside from the fact that clapping rhythms lets us count aloud, clapping is a good way to check the accuracy of ensemble performance. When we strive for real precision, even the simplest rhythm may serve as a valuable study in ensemble. It is surprisingly difficult for fifteen people to clap at exactly the same time.

When we sing the rhythms, we can use any simple syllable that begins with a good definite consonant; "ta" is obvious. For fast patterns, it is easier to alternate syllables: "ta-fa-te-fe" is easier to sing rapidly than "ta-ta-ta-ta." For patterns of eighth-, sixteenth-, and thirty-second-notes, the names of the notes may be spoken or sung in rhythm with one syllable to each note; this can facilitate learning both the sound and the notation of the rhythmic pattern, and introduces nothing that might seem arbitrary and extraneous. If we learn to sing

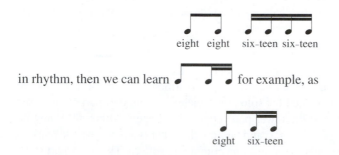

in rhythm, then we can learn ♩ ♩♩ for example, as

eight   six-teen

This system will be discussed further at the beginning of relevant chapters. Several other patterns of rhythmic syllables are in common use. A system used in Kodály practice assigns "ta" to quarters and longer notes, "ti" to eighths, "ti-ri" to two sixteenths, and "tim" and "rim" respectively to dotted eighths beginning on and off the beat:[1]

ta   ti   ti   ti- ri- ti- ri tim - ri

If those studying this book are using a system of rhythmic syllables for music education classes, there may be some point in using that system here.

Conducting the meter helps keep the beat steady and lets the hand take care of counting beats. Most important, it helps us feel the beat and the continuous motion from beat to beat physically, kinetically. We should conduct while singing the one-part rhythms so that conducting becomes natural. Only when we can conduct the patterns for the different meters without thinking about them does conducting become a help. If beating time seems a hindrance rather than a help—one more thing to think about—then it should be practiced assiduously, as it is an essential tool for musicians. However, we must not grow dependent on our hands to keep the beat because they will, in many musical situations, be otherwise occupied, so we should also practice without conducting.

The general tempo indications and the metronome indications of precise tempi given for all the studies should be observed. While they may not always be appropriate for a student's level of skill, the aim should be to perform every study at the given tempo. We do, after all, have to perform both slow music and fast music. Nothing will make the studies more boring than working on them all at the same moderate tempo. (Neither coffee nor lemonade tastes best lukewarm.) As with dynamics, however, the tempo may be varied, if doing so is a conscious creative decision rather than a way to avoid difficulty.

Metronomes are useful for checking steadiness of tempo. In general we should consider a study learned only when we can perform it with a metronome at a tempo close to the one indicated. On the other hand, too much practice with a metronome may foster dependence on it. We must learn to keep a steady beat without such mechanical help. And musical rhythm is not as unrelentingly steady as a metronome, so metronomic regularity cannot be our ultimate goal.

Metronome numbers indicate the number of ticks per minute. Thus longer values are represented by lower numbers. (In a given tempo there are fewer half-notes than eighth-notes per minute.) This principle must be understood in order to figure out equivalences. If the eighth-note is constant at 108, for example, the sixteenth-note, half as long, is at 216, and the quarter-note is at 54; the dotted quarter, three times as long, is a third as fast at 36.

Because of their clear phrase structure, the studies are suitable for dictation. The greatest benefit of dictation, once we know how to write the patterns, is the development of memory. Therefore, one person should sing a phrase until those taking dictation can sing it back; only after they can sing it from memory should they write it. Individuals working alone can develop skill by reading a phrase until it is memorized, and then writing it.

The studies are meant to be *studied,* not just sight-read. Many of them will challenge even experienced musicians. There is no point in studying them unless they are worked to a level of good performance. Unless a rhythm is performed correctly, a different rhythm is heard. Unless two against three is an exactly even two against an exactly even three, the point of the pattern is lost.

Here, then, is an ordered list of ways any study may be learned and performed; it is not expected that all these will be applied to any one study. However, each step chosen should be completed perfectly before proceeding to another. The goal is to achieve a performance that is both accurate and musical.

1. Determine the meter and silently read the rhythm; if beginnings of beats are not obvious, mark them; if any patterns are unfamiliar, isolate them and practice them separately.

2. Determine the phrasing, and mark it if necessary.

3. Check the given tempo with a metronome. While studies may initially be practiced more slowly, the effort should be to achieve facility at the notated tempo.

4. Determine the smallest division of the beat that appears in the study and that is consistent with all patterns, and count aloud, articulating these divisions, listening to the evenness of the counting, silently reading the rhythm.

5. Unless they are indicated, decide dynamic level and shape.

6. Count aloud, articulating the smallest division of the beat that appears in the study and is consistent with all the patterns, while clapping or tapping the rhythm.

7. Count just the beats aloud, listening to the evenness of the counting, while reading the notated rhythm.

8. Clap the rhythm while counting the beats aloud. The point is to hear the pattern of the notated rhythm against the absolute steadiness of the counting, so we need to listen to both, and not drown out the clapping with the counting, or vice versa.

9. Clap the rhythm while counting the beats silently.

10. Conduct the meter while reading the rhythm silently.

11. Choose the pitch(es) for singing, and sing the rhythm while conducting, using some system of rhythmic syllables (perhaps naming the note-values). Work to give each phrase continuity, coherence, and shape.

12. Sing the rhythm on *ta,* at the given tempo and with the intended dynamics, while conducting the meter.

13. Sing the rhythm on *ta,* at the given tempo and with the intended dynamics, without conducting the meter.

14. Perform the study antiphonally, by having one person or group sing each phrase, reading the music, while another repeats each phrase from memory.

15. Memorize at least one phrase, either from dictation or from reading it, and then write it down from memory.

16. Make up a tune that fits the rhythm, and sing or play it.

17. Compose a short rhythmic piece, with or without text, using the rhythmic patterns of the study.

While the chapters are arranged to form a logical progression, and within the chapters the studies are arranged in order of increasing difficulty, it is not necessary to learn all the studies in one chapter before proceeding to the next. To work straight through the book may not be as helpful as to do some of the studies in each chapter and then to return to earlier chapters and work some of the other studies. Performance of complicated rhythmic patterns, changing meters, unequal beats, and cross-rhythms is not learned once and then known forever, any more than is performance of scales; we have to keep practicing.

Understanding the basic processes of musical rhythm is necessary for good musical performance. Musical rhythm is complex and difficult to describe because of the number of factors involved and their interdependence.[2] Rhythm is made by durations of sound and silence and by accent. Accent is made by many factors, of which loudness is just one. Duration makes accent, as a longer note is emphasized by its length, so these two basic factors of rhythm are not separable.

The rhythm in this book, like the rhythm of most Western art music, is metrical. Meter is the grouping by accent of normally regular pulses (beats) into measures beginning with stronger accents. Within the measure, there is a hierarchy of beats and parts of beats, in that some beats are stronger than others, and beats are stronger than half-beats, which are in turn stronger than quarter-beats, and so on. When rhythm is metrical, the rhythmic patterns are heard against a background of regularly recurring pulses and accents. When other kinds of accent, especially stress and duration, do not coincide with metrical accents, the result is syncopation.

Just as one factor of rhythmic pattern, duration, can produce the other factor, accent, rhythmic patterns produce the meter they are heard against. That is, meter is made audible through sounding rhythmic patterns; only after the meter is established will the listener retain it as a set of expectations and hear a rhythmic pattern agree or conflict with it. Much of the fun of metrical rhythm, and its expressive power, derive from the interplay of irregular patterns and metrical regularity, and the performer should enjoy this interplay and project it for the audience to enjoy.

It is common in performance to stress the downbeat slightly. The stress seems especially necessary in performing music where there is no change of pitch. (In much music, the downbeat accent is made by harmonic change, and no additional stress is necessary or desirable.) However, once the meter is established, the listener hears a metrical accent on the downbeat, and the performer must consider the musical context to determine how much dynamic accent, if any, should be added to the metrical accent. A long note has its own accent, and an added dynamic accent may make the note too conspicuous. Too much accent breaks a musical line into pieces. We must be sensitive to accent if our performance is to be musical.

We speak of musical rhythm as composed of various discrete units: beats, measures, patterns of different lengths. But the essential quality of musical rhythm is its ongoingness.[3] The conductor's baton must never stop moving. Most downbeats function both as goal of the preceding measure and as beginning of the new one. Patterns articulate a continuous flow. For rhythm to be music, it must have this flow. We must, while aiming for a correct performance of rhythmic patterns, strive always to create the articulated flow of musical rhythm.

NOTES

[1]Lois Choksy, *The Kodály Context: Creating an Environment for Musical Learning* (Englewood Cliffs, NJ: Prentice-Hall, Inc., 1981), p. 190. On the next page of the book Choksy gives a different system developed by Pierre Perron.

[2]For an extended discussion of the complexity of rhythm, see Wallace Berry, *Structural Functions in Music* (Englewood Cliffs, NJ: Prentice-Hall, 1976), pp. 301–424.

[3]*Cf.* Susanne Langer's assertion that the essential characteristic of any rhythmic motion is that the end of one action is the beginning of the next, in *Problems of Art* (New York: Charles Scribner's Sons, 1957), pp. 50–51.

1. TWO-FOUR METER

This chapter is devoted to two-four time, with no notes shorter than eighth-notes. The relatively simple material allows us to concentrate on the techniques of performing the rhythmic studies: counting aloud while clapping the rhythm, conducting the meter while singing the rhythm, improvising melodies with the rhythm, and so on, as outlined in the Introduction.

Conducting duple meter is rather like bouncing an imaginary ball, with the point of the beat at the point of contact with the ball. On the downbeat, the right hand descends and rebounds away from the body, tracing a backwards J; on the upbeat, the hand moves slightly down and then rebounds up to the original position. To establish the tempo, we conduct just one beat before the first sounding beat. When a piece begins on the downbeat, we begin by conducting an upbeat, and vice versa.

In performing the two-part studies, we should notice the relation between the two parts. Study 1.H is the first of many where one part is an ostinato. Study 1.I is the first of many canons; here the clapped part leads the sung part by one beat.

The notation of rests is often governed by different rules from the notation of notes. A note lasting a whole measure in two-four is a half-note, but a rest lasting a whole measure is a whole rest, as in three-four and four-four and other meters. A number over a whole rest indicates the number of measures of silence.

1. 1) ♩ = 60–160

1. A) Allegro (♩ = 144)

1. B) Allegretto (♩ = 120)

1. C) Presto (♩ = 168)

1. 2) ♩ = 66–160

1.D) Vivo (♩ = 144)

1. E)   Allegretto (♩ = 100)

1. 3)   ♩ = 60–160

1. F)   Andante (♩ = 88)

1. G)   Allegretto (♩ = 108)

1. 4)   ♩ = 72–144

1. H) Moderato (♩ = 100)

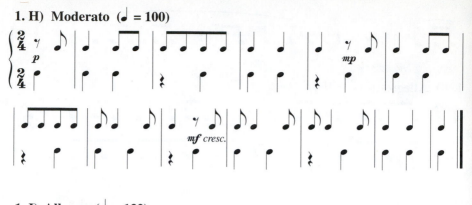

1. I) Allegro (♩ = 132)

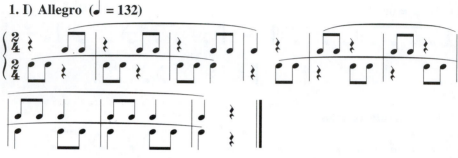

1. J) Andante (♩ = 72)

1. K) Allegro (♩ = 100)

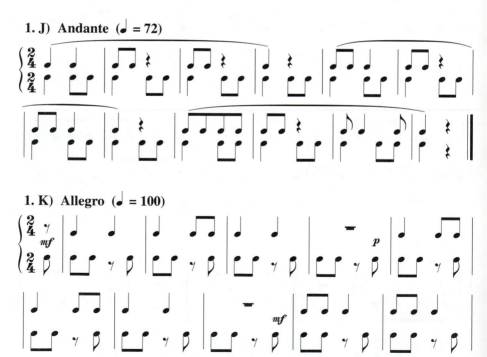

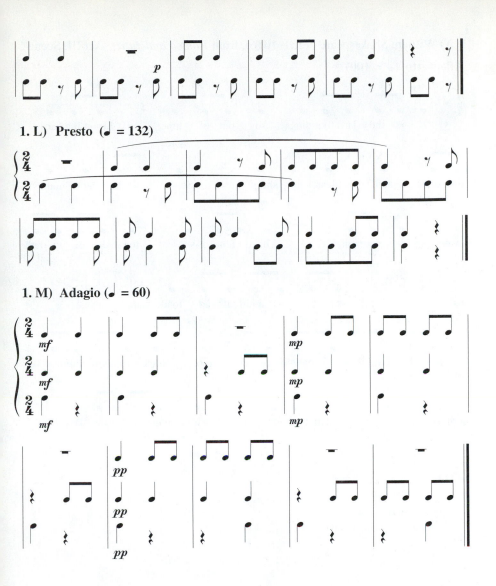

1. L) Presto (♩ = 132)

1. M) Adagio (♩ = 60)

1. N) William Shakespeare (1564–1616), from *Romeo and Juliet,* Act III, Scene 5

Allegretto (♩ = 100)

It is the lark that sings so out of tune, Strain-ing harsh dis-cords and un-pleas - ing sharps. Some say the lark makes sweet di - vi-sion; This doth not so, for she di - vi-deth us. Some say the lark and loath-èd toad chang'd eyes; O, now I would they had chang'd voi-ces too, Since arm from arm that voice doth us af- fray,[1] Hunt-ing thee hence with hunt's-up[2] to the day.

NOTES

[1]disturb, frighten
[2]song to wake up hunters

2. THREE-FOUR METER

Three-four meter is more complex than two-four not only because it has another beat, but because, although the downbeat remains strongest, the relative strengths of the second and third beats may shift. In conducting, the right hand may hook slightly to the left on the downbeat in order to move out to the right on the second beat and diagonally back up to the starting point on the third beat.

Although half-notes are used for two beats in three-four meter, half-rests are not used in this meter: two beats of silence require two quarter rests. A dot extends a note by half the value of the note, so here a dotted half-note is 2 + 1 = 3 beats, constituting a whole measure.

2. 1) ♩ = 84–184

2. A) Allegretto (♩ = 112)

2. B) Allegro (♩ = 168)

2. C) Vivace (♩ = 192)

2. 2) ♩ = 60–160

2. D) Allegro (♩ = 152)

2. E) Andante (♩ = 96)

2. 3) ♩ = 60–160

2. F) Allegretto (♩ = 112)

2. G) Allegro (♩ = 138)

2. 4) ♩ = 60–160

2. H) Allegro (♩ = 168)

2. I) Allegro (♩ = 160)

2. 5) ♩ = 60–126

2. J) Allegretto (♩ = 100)

2. K) Allegro (♩ = 120)

2. L) Vivace (♩ = 138)

2. M) Allegro moderato (♩ = 120)

2. N) Paul Dunbar (1872–1906), "Compensation"

Allegro (♩ = 144)

mf

Be-cause I had loved so deep-ly, Be-cause I had

loved so long, God in His great com - pas-sion

p

Gave me the gift of song. Be-cause I have loved so

vain-ly, And sung with such fal – ter-ing breath, The Mas-ter, in

in – fin – ite mer- cy, Of- fers the boon of death.

3. FOUR-FOUR METER

The signature for four-four meter may be either two fours or **C**. The latter is commonly said to stand for "common time," but this symbol, an incomplete circle, was used in Renaissance notation to designate duple-simple meter.

In some compositions in four-four meter, the first and third quarters are clearly the main strong and weak beats, like the two quarters in two-four. Other times, the four-four measure is more like two two-four measures, and the first and third beats are about equally strong.

In conducting four, the right hand bounces straight up on the downbeat, and moves to the left on the second beat. On the third beat, which is the second strong beat, the hand moves out to the right, and on the last beat, as always, it returns up to the starting point.

In Study 3.E, and in comparable situations, the accent marks indicate just enough impulse to make the downbeat clear when the second beat is accented by a longer note.

3. 1) ♩ = 76–176

3. A) Allegretto (♩ = 108)

3. B) Allegro (♩ = 120)

3. C) Vivace (♩ = 192)

3. 2) ♩ = 60–160

3. D) Andante (♩ = 80)

3. E) Presto (♩ = 160)

3. F) Allegro moderato ($\quarternote$ = 120)

3. 3) $\quarternote$ = 66–168

3. G) Allegretto ($\quarternote$ = 100)

3. H) Vivace ($\quarternote$ = 160)

19

3. 4) ♩ = 60–120

3. I) Vivo (♩ = 144)

3. J) Allegretto (♩ = 88)

3. K) Allegro (♩ = 108)

3. L) Adagio (♩ = 72)

3. M) Edgar Allan Poe (1809–1849), from "The Bells"

Allegro (♩ = 152)

pp

Hear the sled-ges with the bells   Sil-ver bells!   What a world of mer-ri-ment their

, p

mel-o-dy fore-tells! How they tin-kle, tin-kle, tin-kle, In the i-cy air of night! While the

stars that ov-er-sprin-kle All the heav-ens,   seem to   twin-kle With a cry-stal-line de-

mp

light;   Keep-ing time, time, time, In a sort of Ru-nic rhyme, To the

crescendo poco a poco

tin-tin-na-bu-la-tion that so mu-si-cal-ly wells From the bells, bells, bells, bells,

f , mp

Bells, bells, bells From the jing-ling and the tink-ling of the bells.

4. DOTTED QUARTERS AND TIED EIGHTHS IN SIMPLE METER

As a dot extends a note by half the value of the note, a dotted quarter-note represents a quarter extended by an eighth-note:

Dots must be used instead of ties whenever possible. However, it is a rule of notation that only a whole note, a dotted half-note, or a half-note beginning on the second beat may span the middle of a four-four measure. In any more complicated pattern where a note sounds across the beginning of the third beat, that beat must be shown by a note tied to the preceding note. For example, must be written with a tie so the middle of the measure is visible, because writing the third note as a dotted note— —makes the pattern more difficult to read.

In performing dotted notes, counting the divisions of the beat (here, 1 & 2 &, etc.) helps us get the 3:1 ratio of the lengths correct, and conducting helps us feel the beat and place correctly a note that follows off the beat.

4. 1) ♩ = 72–144

4. A) Andante con moto (♩ = 92)

4. B) Allegro (♩ = 120)

4. C) Allegro (♩ = 132)

4. 2) ♩ = 72–144

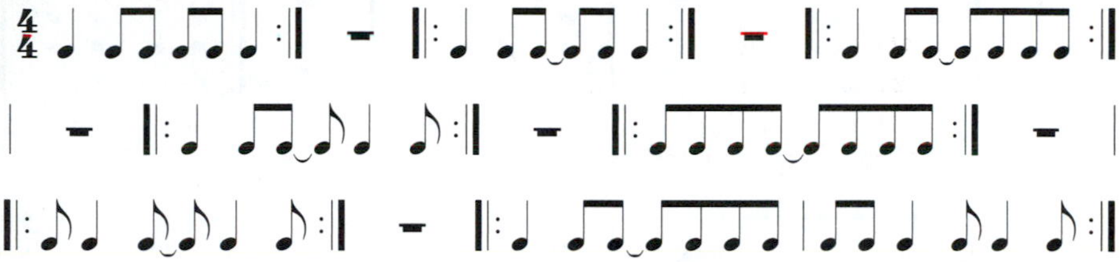

4. D) Allegretto (♩ = 100)

4. E) Vivace (♩ = 152)

4.F) Allegro (♩ = 120)

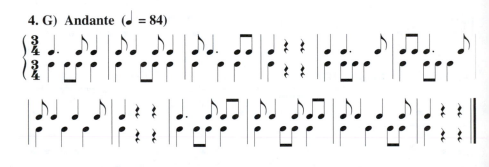

4. 3) ♩ = 60–120

4. G) Andante (♩ = 84)

4. H) Moderato (♩ = 100)

4. I) Andante (♩ = 88)

4. J) Allegro (♩ = 116)

4. K) Allegro moderato (♩ = 112)

4. L) William Shakespeare (1564–1616), from *The Merchant of Venice,*
Act V, Scene 1

Allegretto (♩ = 126)

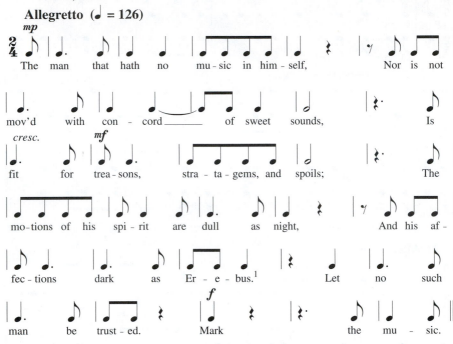

The man that hath no mu-sic in him-self, Nor is not

mov'd with con - cord___ of sweet sounds, Is

cresc.   *mf*

fit for trea-sons, stra - ta - gems, and spoils; The

mo-tions of his spi - rit are dull as night, And his af -

fec - tions dark as Er – e - bus.[1] Let no such

f

man be trust - ed. Mark the mu - sic.

NOTE

[1]dark region under the earth before the entrance to Hades

5. SIX-EIGHT METER

Six-eight is a compound meter, which means that the main division of the beat is by three. A meter is compound when the numerator of the signature is a multiple of three. To find the number of beats in a measure of a compound meter, we divide the numerator by three. As $6 \div 3 = 2$, six-eight is a duple meter, with two beats in a measure. The denominator of the signature names the triple division of the beat, so in six-eight there are three eighth-notes to a beat, and the beat is a dotted quarter.

Because it is a duple meter, we usually count six-eight in two, and when we articulate the divisions of the beat, we still usually count in two: 1 & e 2 & e, and so on. Except in very slow tempi, six-eight is conducted in two. This is why tempi are given for the dotted quarter rather than the eighth-note.

When the tempo is so slow that the measure is conducted in six, one of the common beat patterns is a modification of the four-beat pattern, with the right hand moving to the left for both the second and third beats, and out to the right for both the fourth and fifth beats: down-left-left-right-right-up.

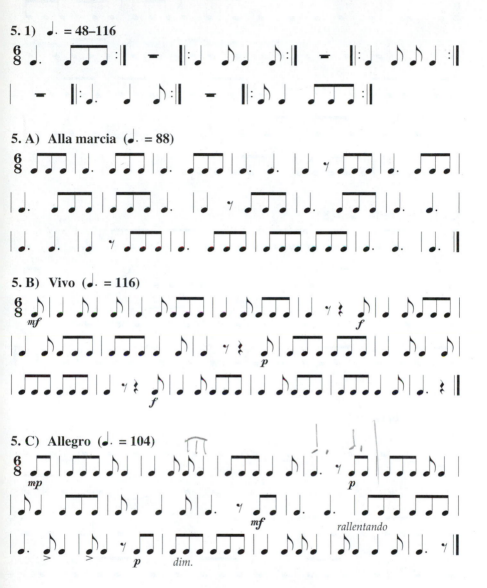

5. 1) ♩. = 48–116

5. A) Alla marcia (♩. = 88)

5. B) Vivo (♩. = 116)

5. C) Allegro (♩. = 104)

5. D) Vivace (♩. = 120)

5. E) Allegretto (♩. = 84)

5. F) Presto (♩. = 126)

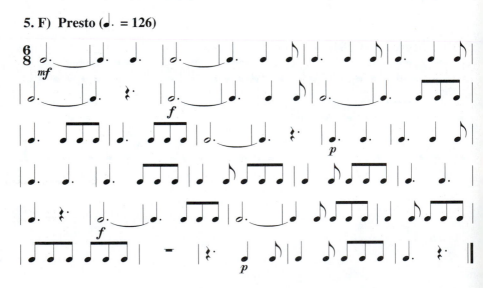

5. 2) ♩. = 48–100

5. G) Allegretto (♩. = 88)

5. H) Andante (♩. = 69)

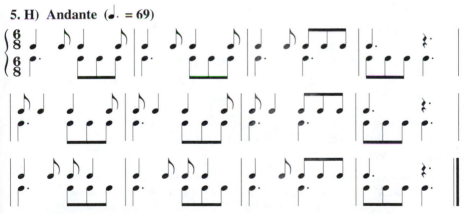

5. I) Allegretto (♩. = 84)

5. J) Andante (♩. = 66)

5. K) Allegretto (♩. = 60)

5. L) Oscar Wilde (1856–1900), from "A Harmony"

Andante (♩. = 72)

Her i-vo-ry hands on the i-vo-ry keys Strayed in a fit-ful fan-ta-sy, Like the

sil-ver gleam when the pop-lar trees Rus-tle their pale leaves list-less-ly, Or the

drift-ing foam of a rest-less sea when the Waves show their teeth in the fly-ing breeze.

6. SIXTEENTH-NOTES IN SIMPLE METER

In learning sixteenth-note patterns, speaking the names of the notes in rhythm reinforces the correlation between the sound of patterns and their notation:

eight   six - teen   six - teen eight   six eight   teen   six - teen   six - teen

"Eight" and "sixteen" are easier to repeat rapidly than "eighth" and "sixteenth." "Six" names the first or accented of two sixteenth-notes, "teen" names the second, unaccented one. This system is less satisfactory for quarters and dotted quarters because the two or three syllables in their names must be sung as eighth-notes:

quarter eight eight quarter dot eight   *is sung as*   quar-ter eight eight quar-ter   dot eight

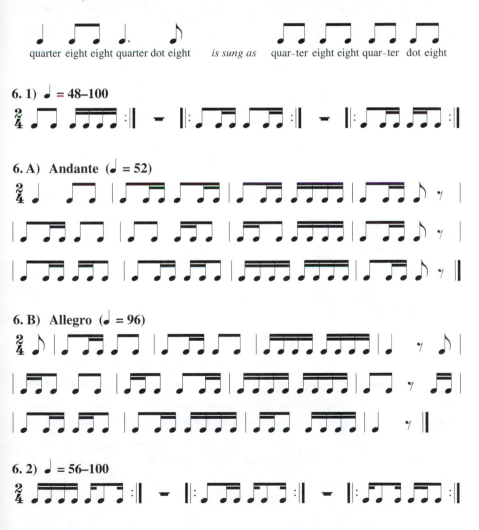

6. 1) ♩ = 48–100

6. A) Andante (♩ = 52)

6. B) Allegro (♩ = 96)

6. 2) ♩ = 56–100

6. C) Allegro ma non troppo, leggiero (♩ = 84)

6. D) Andante (♩ = 72)

6. E) Allegro (♩ = 96)

6. F) Presto (♩ = 108)

6. 3) ♩ = 40–80

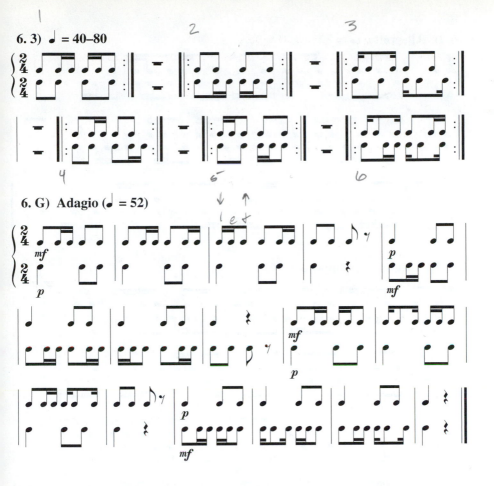

6. G) Adagio (♩ = 52)

6. H) Andante (♩ = 60)

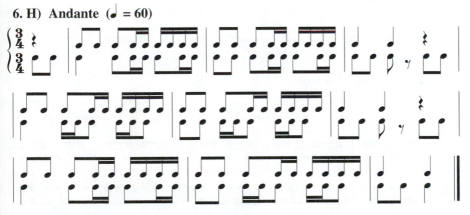

6. I) Allegretto (♩ = 72)

6. J) Allegro non troppo (♩ = 76)

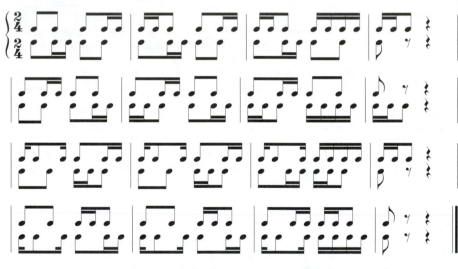

6. K) Andantino (♩ = 60)

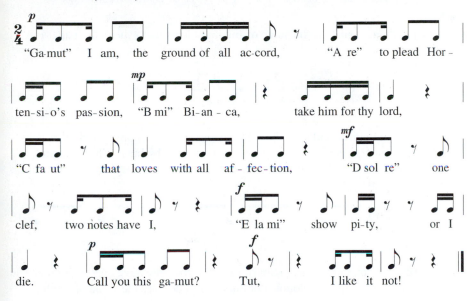

6. L) William Shakespeare (1564–1616), from *The Taming of the Shrew,*
Act III, Scene 1

> Hortensio: Madam, before you touch the instrument
> To learn the order of my fingering
> I must teach you the rudiments of art,
> To teach you gamut in a briefer sort . . . [1]

Andantino (♩ = 72)

p
"Ga-mut" I am, the ground of all ac-cord, "A re" to plead Hor -

mp
ten-si-o's pas-sion, "B mi" Bi-an - ca, take him for thy lord,

mf
"C fa ut" that loves with all af - fec-tion, "D sol re" one

f
clef, two notes have I, "E la mi" show pi-ty, or I

p   *f*
die. Call you this ga-mut? Tut, I like it not!

NOTE

[1]Hortensio is here courting Bianca. His gamut, or scale, that Bianca reads was given an elaborate explanation by Henry Collin Miller in "A Shakespearean Music Lesson" (*Notes and Queries,* 165 [1933]: 255–57). As with "Doh, a deer," there is a series of puns, of which the least obscure to modern ears, if *mi* is pronounced as "my," are "B mi Bianca" and "E la mi show pity," which can be heard respectively as "Be my Bianca" and "Ill am I, show pity."

7. DOTTED EIGHTHS IN SIMPLE METER

Since a dot adds to a note half of its value, a dot adds to an eighth-note the value of a sixteenth-note:

In speaking these patterns in the manner explained at the beginning of Chapter 6, the dot may be spoken or the syllable "eight" may be given its extra length: saying "dot" reminds us of the notation but the extra syllable requires an extra note:

eight dot teen six eight dot   *is sung as*   eight dot teen six eight dot

Simply extending "eight" by the value of the dot allows us to speak the pattern in its rhythm:

eight   teen six eight

Counting aloud, articulating the subdivisions, while clapping the rhythm is useful in learning the relative lengths of the notes in dotted rhythms. While clapping, we first count saying syllables for the sixteenths, then only for the eighths, and finally we just count the beats:

1 e & e 2 e & e   1   &   2   &   1   2

The double dot, introduced in Study 7.C, adds to a note three quarters of its value (half plus half of the half); the double dot thus almost doubles the value of a note:

7. 1) $\bullet$ = 52 - 100

7. A) Allegretto (♩ = 72)

7. B) Allegro (♩ = 100)

7. C) Andante con moto (♩ = 63)

7. D) Allegro ma non troppo (♩ = 104)

7. E) Allegretto (♩ = 80)

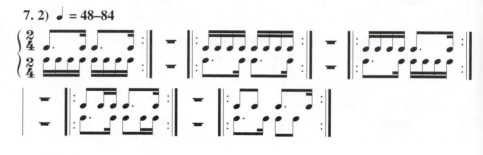

7. 2) ♩ = 48–84

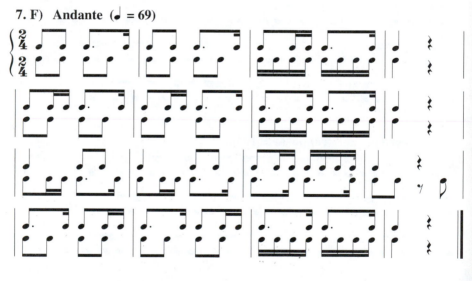

7. F) Andante (♩ = 69)

7. G) Andante (♩ = 66)

38

7. 3) ♩ = 48–84

7. H) Andante (♩ = 60)

7. I) Allegretto (♩ = 76)

7. J) Adagio (♩ = 60)

7. K) Elizabeth Barrett Browning (1806–1861), from "A Musical Instrument"

Allegretto (♩ = 72)

He tore out a reed, the great god Pan, From the deep cool bed of the ri-ver; And

poco a poco crescendo

hacked and hewed as a great god can, With his hard bleak steel at the pa-tient reed, Till

there was not a sign of the leaf in-deed, To prove it fresh from the ri-ver.

"This is the way," laughed the great god Pan (Laughed while he sat by the ri-ver), Then

drop-ping his mouth to a hole in the reed, He blew in pow-er by the ri-ver.

Sweet, sweet sweet, O Pan! Pierc-ing sweet by the ri-ver!

8. SIXTEENTH-NOTES IN SIX-EIGHT METER

Twenty-four different patterns of sixteenth-notes, eighth-notes, and dotted eighths constitute a dotted-quarter beat in compound time. Performing the patterns by speaking the note-values in rhythm is a good way to become familiar with them:

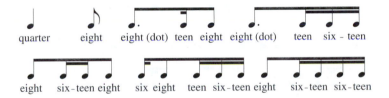

When learning six-eight patterns, we may first count the eighths and articulate the sixteenths, while clapping the rhythm, but we then proceed to count the beats and articulate the eighths, and finally we just count the beats:

The convention of notation that sixteenth-notes within a beat be beamed together makes it difficult in some patterns to see the basic three eighth-notes of the dotted-quarter beat. ♪· ♪♪♪ has to be understood as ♪· ♪♪♪, for example.

In Exercise 8.3, voice and hands reverse parts within each measure. Therefore, the single beats should be practiced until they can be performed easily; only then should whole measures be attempted.

8. 1) (♩. = 40–76)

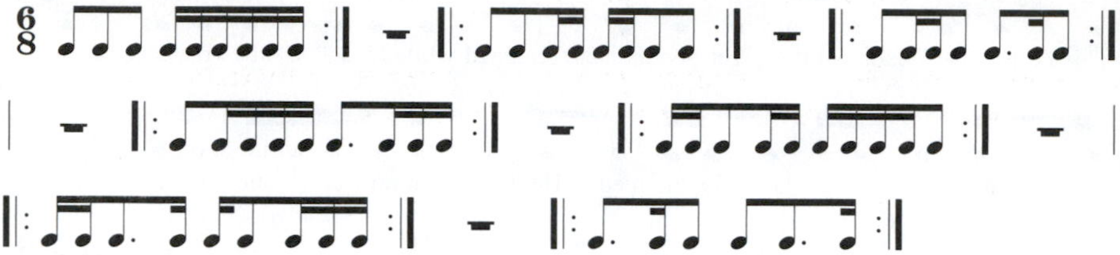

8. A) Grazioso (♩. = 66)

8. B) Adagio (♩. = 52)

8. C) Allegro (♩. = 88)

8. D) Allegretto (♩. = 66)

42

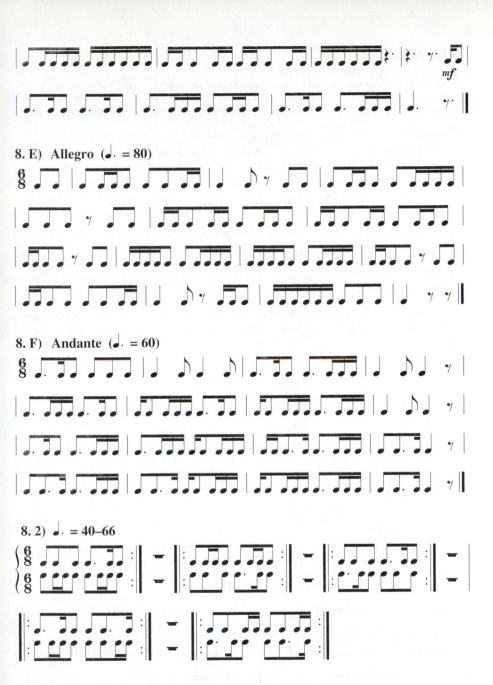

8. E) Allegro (♩. = 80)

8. F) Andante (♩. = 60)

8. 2) ♩. = 40–66

8. G) Allegro (♩. = 88)

8. H) Andante (♩. = 48)

8. 3) ♩. = 40–60

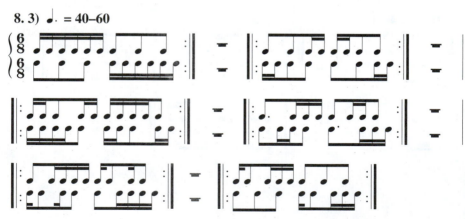

8. I) Allegretto (♩. = 56)

8. J) Adagio (♩. = 44)

8. K) Allegretto (♩. = 56)

8. L) Thomas Hardy (1840–1928), from "A Musical Incident"

Andantino ($\downarrow\cdot = 66$)

'Twas thus. One of them played To please her friend, not know-ing That friend was speed - i - ly grow-ing, Be-hind the play-er's chair, Som - no-lent, un - a - ware Of an-y mu - sic there. "Beau - ti-ful!" said she, wak - ing As the mu-sic ceased. "Heart - ach - ing!" Though ne-ver a note she'd heard To judge of as a - verred - Save that of the ve - ry last word.

9. MORE RESTS AND SYNCOPATION IN SIMPLE METER

In performing a phrase that contains rests, we should still aim to understand and project the whole phrase. Rests interrupt the sound, but they should not interrupt the flow of the phrase.

In this chapter and again in Chapter 10, three of the studies are written with flags instead of beams. This notation is sometimes encountered in vocal music, where notes sung to different syllables may not be connected with beams. The first step in reading such notation is to bracket the notes of beats where the beats are not obvious.

9. 1) $\downarrow = 80$–144

9. A) Allegretto ($\downarrow = 88$)

9. B) Vivace (♩ = 132)

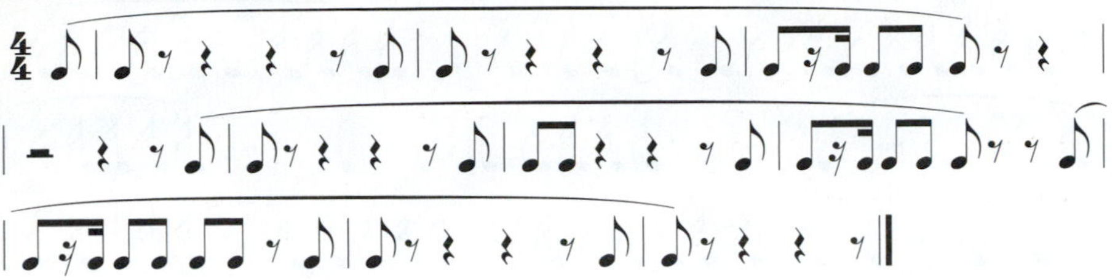

9. C) Moderato (♩ = 84)

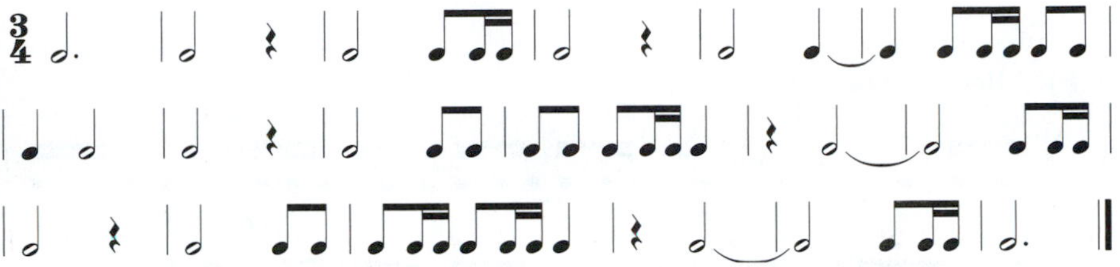

9. 2) ♩ = 56 - 96

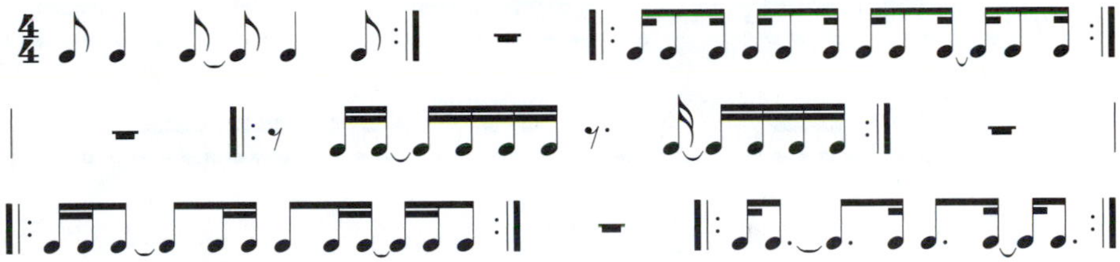

9. D) Allegretto (♩ = 80)

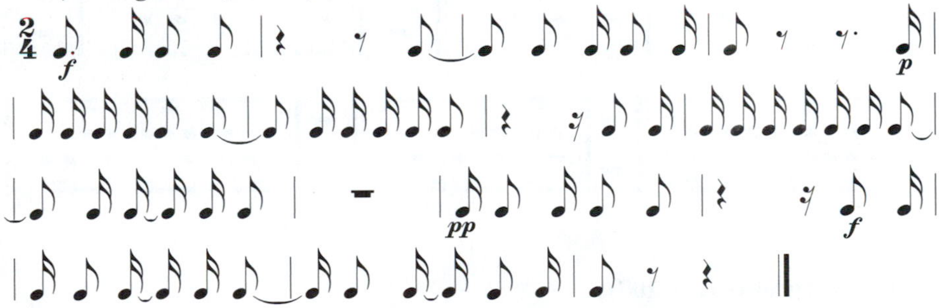

9. E) Allegro (♩ = 96)

9. F) Allegretto (♩ = 72)

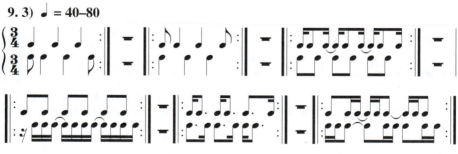

9. 3) ♩ = 40–80

9. G) Allegretto (♩ = 100)

9. H) Moderato ($\quarternote = 69$)

9. I) Allegro ($\quarternote = 92$)

9. J) Allegretto ($\quarternote = 72$)

9. K) Allegro (♩ = 100)

9. L) Ralph Waldo Emerson (1803–1882), from "Music"

Andante (♩ = 63)

pp

'Tis not in the high stars — a - lone, Nor in the cup of bud-ding

flow-ers, Nor in the red-breast's mel-low tone, Nor in the bow that smiles in

show-ers, But in the mud and scum of things There al-way,

al-way some - thing sings.

10. MORE RESTS AND SYNCOPATION IN SIX-EIGHT METER

  Because the beats have more divisions in compound meter than in simple meter, tapping the eighth-note or using a metronome set at the speed of the eighth, until the patterns are thoroughly familiar, may be especially helpful in ensuring correct performance.

  Rewriting Studies 10.B and 10.C using beams may be instructive.

  Three different ways of notating the duple division of the dotted-quarter-note beat are shown in Exercise 10.2.

10. 1) ♩. = 40–72

10. A) Vivo (♩. = 108)

10. B) Allegretto (♩. = 66)

10. C) Allegro (♩. = 72)

10. D) Adagio (♩. = 40)

10. 2) ♩. = 54–96

10. E) Allegretto (♩. = 60)

10. F) Allegro (♩. = 88)

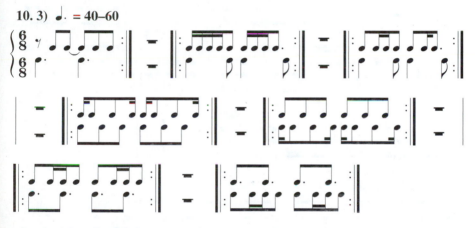

10. 3) ♩. = 40–60

10. G) Allegretto (♩. = 56)

54

10.K) Adagio (♩. = 54)

10. L) Langston Hughes (1902–1967), "Sport"[1]

NOTE

[1]From COLLECTED POEMS by Langston Hughes. Copyright © 1994 by the Estate of Langston Hughes. Reprinted by permission of Alfred A. Knopf Inc.

11. NINE-EIGHT AND TWELVE-EIGHT METER

Nine-eight and twelve-eight meter combine the compound beat patterns of six-eight with the three and four beats of three-four and four-four meter, so there are no new problems here. In Exercise 11.3 especially, single beats should be repeated until they seem easy before whole measures are attempted.

11. 1) ♩. = 40–66

11. A) Allegro vivo (♩. = 120)

11. B) Con moto (♩. = 60)

11. C) Allegretto (♩. = 63)

11. 2) ♩. = 56–76

11. D) Allegro maestoso (♩. = 104)

11. E) Andante con moto (♩. = 66)

11. F) Andante (♩. = 56)

11. 3) ♩. = 40–60

11. G) Allegro non troppo (♩. = 88)

11. H) Andante (♩. = 56)

58

11. I) Allegretto (♩. = 60)

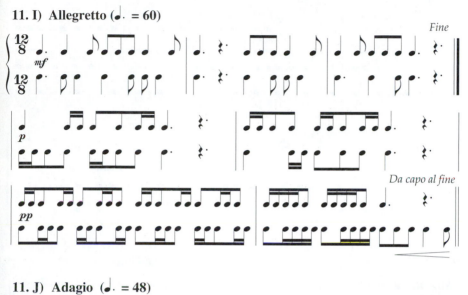

Fine

Da capo al fine

11. J) Adagio (♩. = 48)

11. K) Allegro ($\bullet$. = 112)

11. L) Percy Bysshe Shelley (1792–1822), from "With a Guitar, to Jane"

Adagio ($\bullet$. = 52)

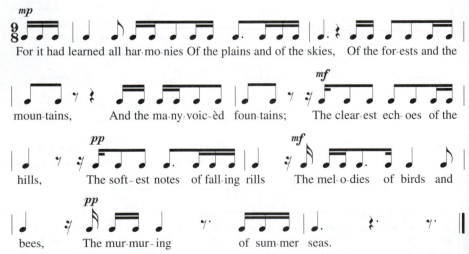

For it had learned all har-mo-nies Of the plains and of the skies,   Of the for-ests and the

moun-tains,   And the ma-ny-voic-èd foun-tains;   The clear-est ech-oes of the

hills,   The soft-est notes   of fall-ing rills   The mel-o-dies   of birds and

bees,   The mur-mur-ing   of sum-mer seas.

12. TRIPLETS

The division of the beat into thirds is familiar from compound meter, and successive performance of duple and triple divisions of the beat was encountered in Chapter 10. The new problems here are dividing into thirds a beat normally divided in half, and performing in succession triple and quadruple divisions of the beat. Successions of eighths, triplets, and sixteenths may be performed by numbering aloud the notes on each beat:

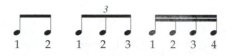

When alternating different divisions of the beat, it is helpful to use a metronome enough to ensure that the beat stays constant.

A common tendency, when moving from duplet to triplet eighth-notes, is to make the first note of a triplet too long. It may help to realize that a third of a beat is closer in length to a quarter of a beat than to half a beat, so triplet eighths are more like sixteenth-notes in length than they are like eighth-notes. When beginning a triplet after a duplet, we must move quickly to its second note, rather than sit on the first note.

In simple meter a sextuplet of sixteenths is usually considered to be two sixteenth-note triplets unless the beams indicate an eighth-note triplet divided into sixteenths.

12. 1) ♩ = 60–120

12. A) Allegro (♩ = 120)

12. B) Allegro ma non troppo (♩ = 112)

12. C) Moderato (♩ = 88)

12. D) Andante con moto (♩ = 76)

12. 2) ♩ = 60–100

12. E) Andante (♩ = 66)

12. F) Allegro (♩ = 100)

12.3) ♩ = 50–80

12. G) Allegretto (♩ = 72)

12. H) Allegretto (♩ = 63)

12. 4) ♩ = 48– 84

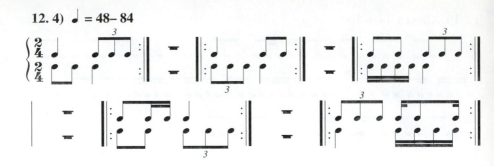

12. I)   Andante (♩ = 80)

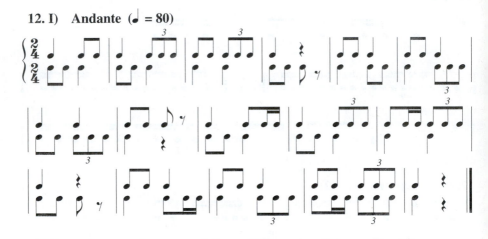

12. J) Andante (♩ = 60)

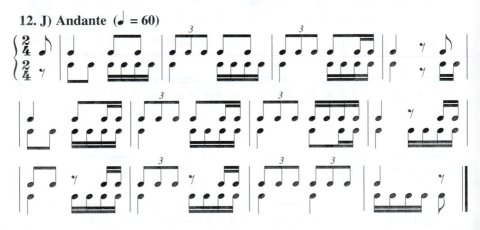

12. K) Con moto (♩ = 72)

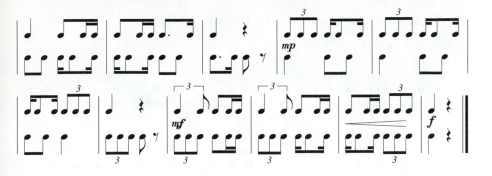

12. L) Allegro ma non troppo (♩ = 112)

12. M) Allegro (♩ = 120)

12. N) Gerard Manley Hopkins (1844–1889), from "Spring"

Noth-ing is so beau-ti-ful as Spring– When weeds, in wheels, shoot

long and love-ly and lush; Thrush's eggs look lit- tle low heav-ens,

and thrush Through the ech - o - ing tim-ber does so

rinse and wring The ear, it strikes like light- nings to hear him sing . . .

13. TWO AGAINST THREE

We encountered two against three in Chapter 10, in the division of the dotted-quarter beat of six-eight meter into two dotted eighth-notes that are heard against the basic triple division of the beat. Review of Exercises 10.2 and 10.3 and Studies 10.E, F, and J provides good preparation for the material in this chapter.

To perform cross-rhythms we must understand the numerical relations of the note-values. When triplet eighths sound against duplet eighths, each note of the triplet is two sixths of a beat, so the triplet eighths begin on the first, third, and fifth sixths of the beat, while the duplet eighths, each three sixths of a beat, begin on the first and fourth sixths of the beat. Grasping the patterns may be facilitated by speaking verbal phrases that we naturally speak in these rhythms:

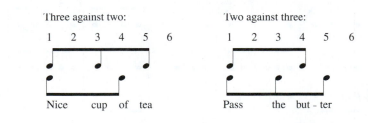

It is relatively easy to hear and perform the composite pattern made by two against three, as the rhythm of the pattern—♩ ♪♪♪—is familiar. However, it is musically important to be able to hear the duplet and triplet as independent concurrent patterns. For this reason, we need to practice two against three slowly so as to hear that the composite pattern is correct *and* quickly so that we can hear two and three at the same time but independent of each other.

13. 1) ♩. = 40–69

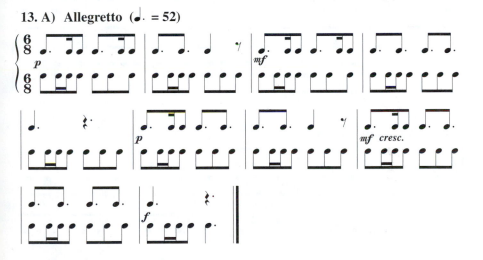

13. A) Allegretto (♩. = 52)

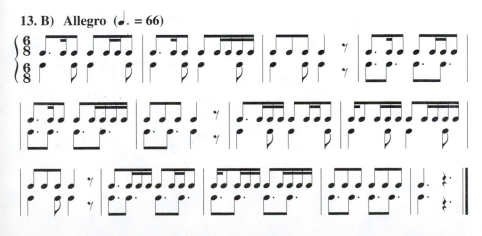

13. B) Allegro (♩. = 66)

13. 2) ♩ = 52– 88

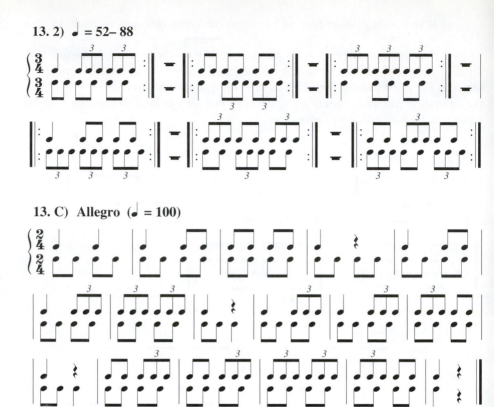

13. C) Allegro (♩ = 100)

13. D) Allegretto (♩ = 80)

13. 3) ♩ = 48–96

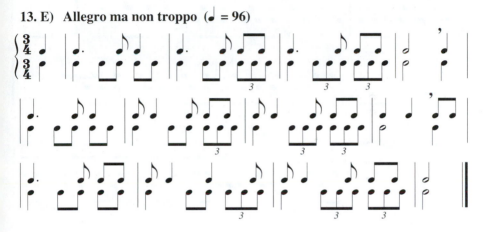

13. E)   Allegro ma non troppo (♩ = 96)

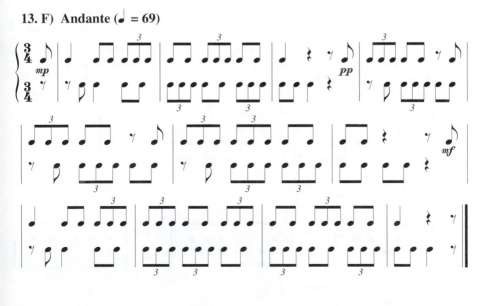

13. F)   Andante (♩ = 69)

13. G) Andantino ($\frac{3}{4}\,\downarrow = \frac{9}{8}\,\downarrow\cdot = 69$)

13. H) Allegretto ($\downarrow = 84$)

13. 4) $\downarrow = 50$–80

13. I) Allegretto (♩ = 72)

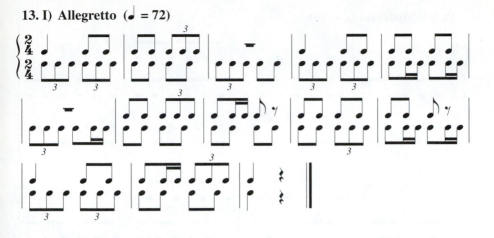

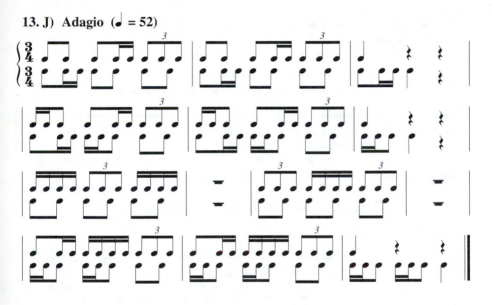

13. J) Adagio (♩ = 52)

13. K) Moderato ($\bullet$ = 76)

13. L)   Langston Hughes (1902–1967), from "The Weary Blues"[1]

Andante ($\bullet$ = 66)

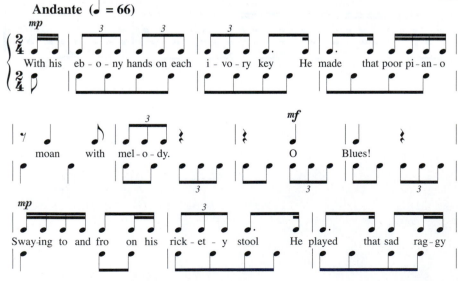

With his eb - o - ny hands on each i - vo - ry key   He made   that poor pi - an - o

moan   with mel - o - dy.   O   Blues!

Sway-ing to and fro on his rick - et - y stool   He played   that sad   rag - gy

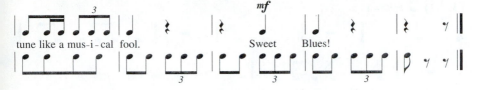

tune like a mus-i-cal fool.   Sweet   Blues!

NOTE

[1]From COLLECTED POEMS by Langston Hughes. Copyright © 1994 by the Estate of Langston Hughes. Reprinted by permission of Alfred A. Knopf Inc.

14. HALF-NOTE BEAT

When no values smaller than eighth-notes are involved, the half-note beat presents no new rhythmic difficulties, but simply a problem of reading: we must *see* a half-note as one beat, a whole note as only two beats, and a quarter-note as half a beat. The first two exercises that follow (14.1 and 14.2) are given first in four-four meter and then in four-two; the performance of the two versions should be identical. Likewise, the first study (14.A) is given first in two-four, then in two-two meter, and the two versions should sound the same. Rewriting the next three studies may help make the simplicity of the rhythm obvious.

Sixteenth-notes, which appear in Exercise 14.3 and the following studies, divide the half-note beat into eight parts. Saying the names of the note-values in rhythm while beating time may be helpful in learning to feel this division:

eight   eight   eight   eight   six - teen   six - teen   six - teen   six - teen

The division of the beat into eight will be encountered again when thirty-second-notes appear in quarter-note beats in Chapter 18.

As **C** stands for four-four meter, **¢** stands for two-two. The symbol appearing at the beginning of Study 14.H is the breve, which equals two whole notes. Originally a square note, it is now written as a whole note between two vertical lines. The breve rest is used less often than the whole rest for a whole measure of silence, even when the measure is longer than a whole note, and even though the whole rest is also used for a half-measure rest in four-two time, as in Study 14.C. Two half-rests, not a whole rest, are used for two beats in three-two time, just as quarter rests, not a half rest, are used for two beats in three-four time.

14. 1.1) ♩ = 88–176

14. 1.2) ♩ = 88–176

14. A.1) Allegro (♩ = 132)

mp

mf

p

mf

14. A.2) Allegro (♩ = 132)

mp

mf

p

mf

14. B) Presto (♩ = 160)

14. F) Largo ($\textit{d}$ = 44)

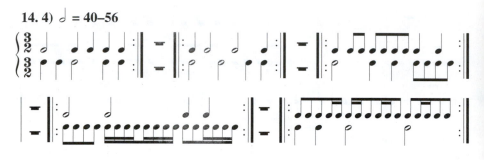

morendo

14. 4) $\textit{d}$ = 40–56

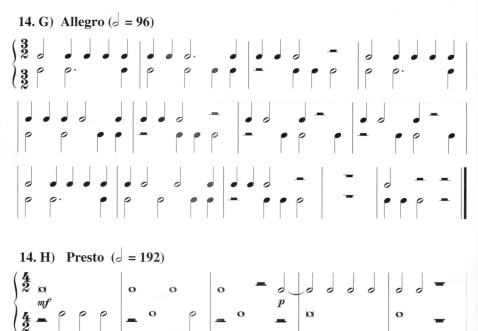

14. G) Allegro ($\textit{d}$ = 96)

14. H)   Presto ($\textit{d}$ = 192)

14. I) Allegro ma non troppo (♩ = 104)

14. J) Adagio (♩ = 40)

14. K) Andante (= 72)

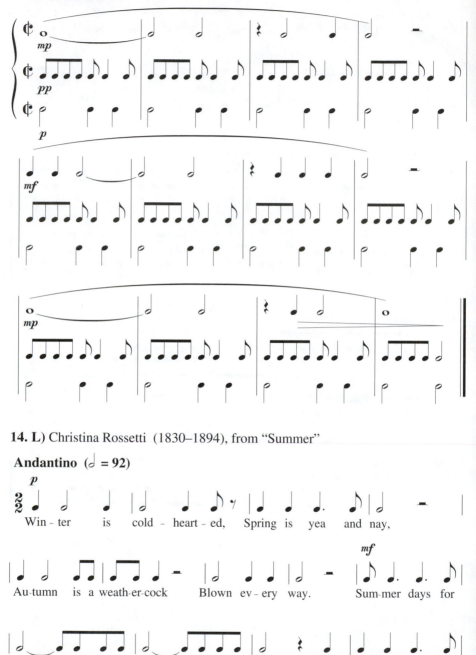

14. L) Christina Rossetti (1830–1894), from "Summer"

Andantino (= 92)

Win - ter   is   cold - heart - ed,   Spring is   yea   and nay,

Au-tumn   is a weath-er-cock   Blown ev - ery way.   Sum-mer days for

me   When eve-ry   leaf   is on its   tree;   When Rob-in's   not   a

crescendo

beg-gar, And Jen-ny Wren's a bride, And larks hang sing-ing, sing-ing,

f   *mf*

sing – ing, O – ver the wheat-fields wide, And an-chored li-lies

mp   ⌐ 3 ⌐

ride, And the pen-du-lum spi – der swings from side to side.

15. DOTTED-HALF-NOTE BEAT

Reading six-four and nine-four meter, we quickly appreciate the clarity with which beams show beats in six-eight and nine-eight meter. Here, we have to learn to see nine consecutive quarter-notes as constituting three beats. Exercise 15.1 is written first in nine-eight; the nine-four version should sound the same.

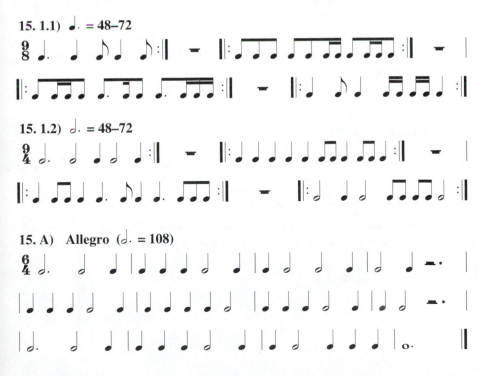

15. 1.1) ♩. = 48–72

15. 1.2) ♩. = 48–72

15. A) Allegro (♩. = 108)

15. B) Adagio ($\textit{d.} = 56$)

15. C) Vivace ($\textit{d.} = 126$)

15. D) Andante ($\textit{d.} = 60$)

15. E) Allegro ($\textit{d.} = 72$)

15. 2) ♩. = 40–60

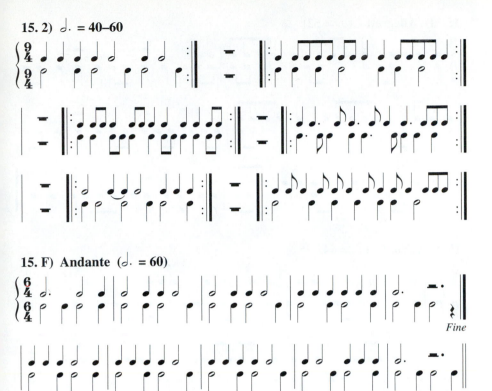

15. F) Andante (♩. = 60)

Fine

Da capo

15. G) Moderato (♩. = 72)

15. H) Allegretto ($\downarrow$. = 52)

15. I) Andante ($\downarrow$. = 44)

15. J) Maestoso ($\downarrow$. = 72)

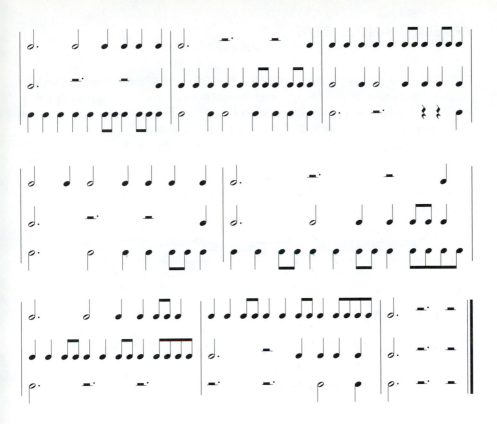

15. K) John Greenleaf Whittier (1807–1892), from *"Laus Deo! On Hearing the Bells Ring on the Passage of the Constitutional Amendment Abolishing Slavery"*

Maestoso (♩. = 54)

f

It is done! Clang of bell and roar of gun Send the tid-ings up and down. How the bel-fries rock and reel! How the great guns, peal on peal, Fling _ the joy from town to town! Ring, O bells! Ev-ery stroke ex-ul-ting tells Of the bu-ri-al hour of crime. Loud _ and long, that all may hear. Ring _ for ev-ery lis-ten-ing ear Of E-ter-ni-ty and Time!

16. EIGHTH-NOTE BEAT

There are no new rhythmic problems here, but simply the problem of seeing a quarter-note as equal to two beats, an eighth-note as equal to a beat, a sixteenth-note as equal to half a beat, and so on. Exercise 16.1 is written first in four-four time to show how much easier the rhythm looks in the more familiar meter.

The four syllables of "thirty-second" may be spoken evenly so as to match the four thirty-second notes within the time of an eighth-note. Although the syllables become too tricky to be useful in some dotted and syncopated patterns, speaking the names of the note-values may be helpful in learning the more straightforward patterns of eighths, sixteenths, and thirty-seconds:

16. 1.1) ♩ = 72–112

16. 1.2) ♪ = 72–112

16. A)   Allegretto (♪ = 112)

16. B) Vivace (♪ = 120)

16. C) Presto (♪ = 184)

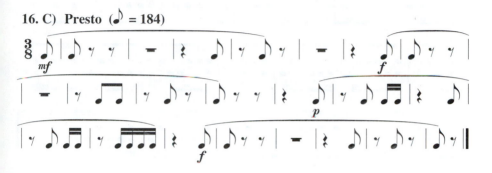

16. D) Largo (♪ = 60)

16. E) Allegretto (♪ = 92)

16. F) Allegretto (♪ = 112)

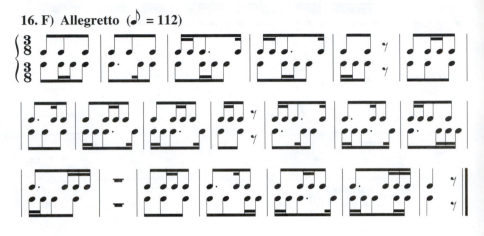

16. G) Allegro (♪ = 120)

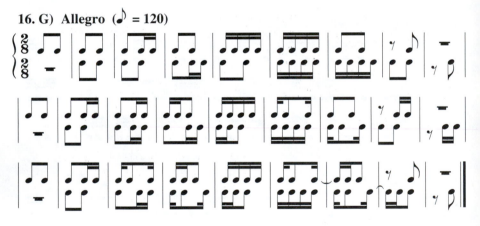

16. H) Adagio ($\flat$ = 56)

16. I) Allegretto ($\flat$ = 96)

16. J) Largo (♪ = 50)

16. K) William Shakespeare (1564–1616), from *King Richard II,* Act 5, Scene 5

Allegro moderato ($\flat$ = 88)

mf

Ha, ha, keep time! How sour sweet mu – sic is When time is broke, and

no pro-por-tion kept! So— is it in the mu – sic of men's lives. And

crescendo   *mf*

here have I the daint-i-ness of ear To check time broke in a dis-or-der'd

string; But for the con-cord of my state and time, Had not an ear to

f   *mp*   *diminuendo*   *pp*

hear my true time broke. I wast-ed time, and now doth time waste me.

17. DOTTED-EIGHTH-NOTE BEAT

Again, the problem here is one of reading. In order to read six-sixteen or nine-sixteen meter, we must be able to see a dotted quarter as two beats and ♩♩ as a complete beat.

Exercise 17.1 is presented first in the more familiar nine-eight meter.

17. 1.1) ♩. = 44–76

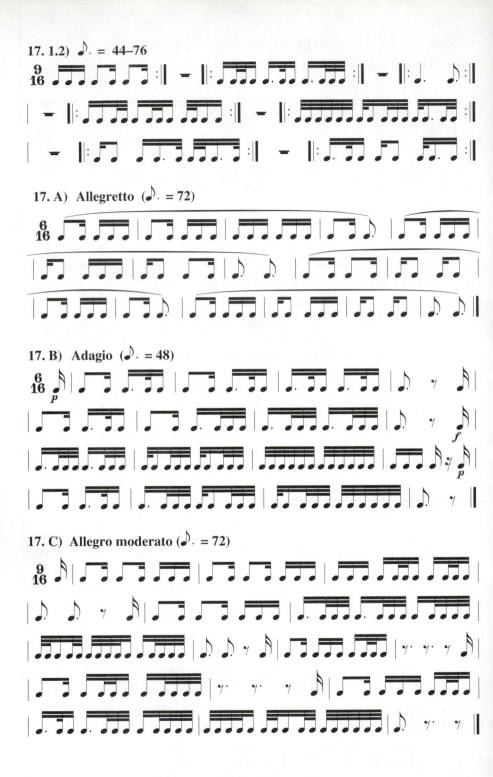

17. 1.2) ♪. = 44–76

17. A) Allegretto (♪. = 72)

17. B) Adagio (♪. = 48)

17. C) Allegro moderato (♪. = 72)

17. D) Allegretto (♪. = 63)

17. E) Allegro ma non troppo (♪. = 88)

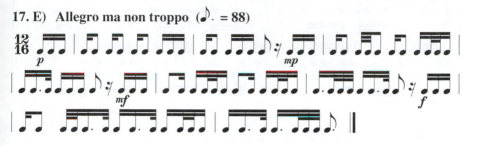

17. 2) ♪. = 40–60

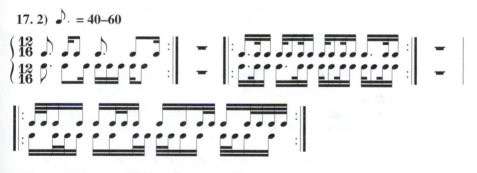

17. F) Allegro (♪. = 92)

91

17. G) Vivo (♪. = 138)

17. H) Andante (♪. = 56)

Fine

Da capo al fine

17. I) Andante (♪. = 54)

17. J) John Dryden (1631–1700), from "A Song for St. Cecilia's Day"

Allegretto (♩. = 88)

What pas-sion can-not Mu-sic raise and quell! When Ju-bal struck the cor-ded

shell, His lis-ten-ing breth-ren stood a-round, And, won-der-ing, on their fa-ces fell

To wor-ship that ce-les-tial sound. Less than a god they thought there could not

dwell With-in the hol-low of that shell That spoke so sweet-ly and so well. What

pas-sion can-not Mu-sic raise and quell!

18. SMALL SUBDIVISIONS

We encountered thirty-second-notes in two-eight and three-eight meter; we encountered division of the beat into eight when sixteenth-notes appeared in a half-note beat. Only sixty-fourth-notes, dividing the quarter-note beat into sixteen, are new here. Such small subdivisions occur in slow tempi and are often ornamental; they should be sung lightly and easily.

The more complicated single-beat patterns should be learned before whole measures are attempted. If we want to count divisions of the beat while clapping the rhythm, or to tap divisions while singing the rhythm, we must figure out what division will be useful. In the fifth segment of Exercise 18.1, for example, sixteenth-note sextuplets will fit the patterns on all three beats, but in the sixth segment of the same exercise, where the eighth-note is divided into both two and three sixteenths, the smallest practical common division of the beat is the eighth-note. With Study 18.A, it can help to tap sixteenths until the patterns are easy, and then eighths, before conducting in three. Tapping steady eighth-notes is helpful in approaching Study 18.C in spite of the occasional eighth-note triplets.

18. 1) ♩ = 40–60

18. A) Largo (♩ = 48)

18. B) Adagio (♩ = 52)

18. C) Largo (♩ = 48)

18. 2) ♪ = 44–60

18. D) Lento (♪ = 60)

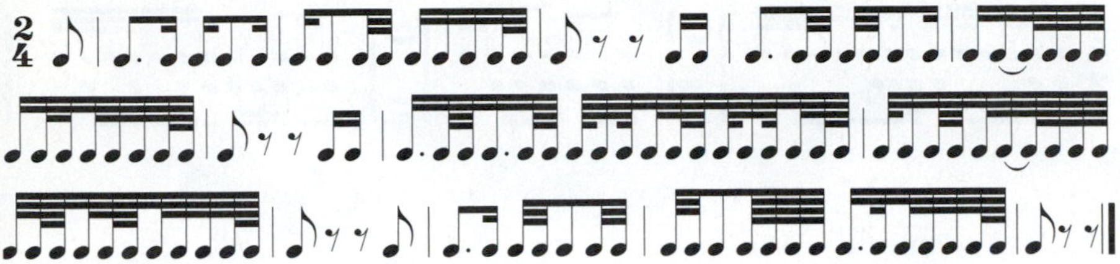

18. 3) ♪ = 80–108

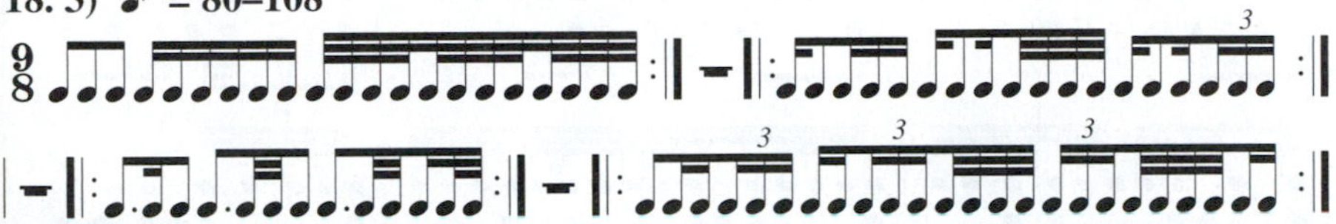

18. E) Lento (♩. = 40)

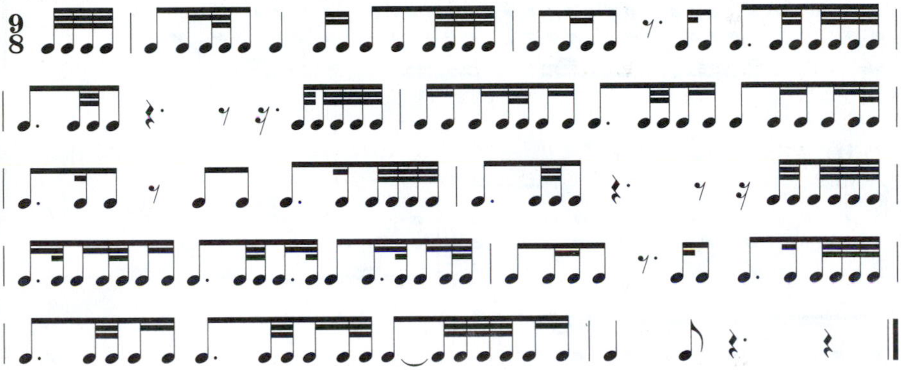

18. F) Andante (♩. = 36, ♪ = 108)

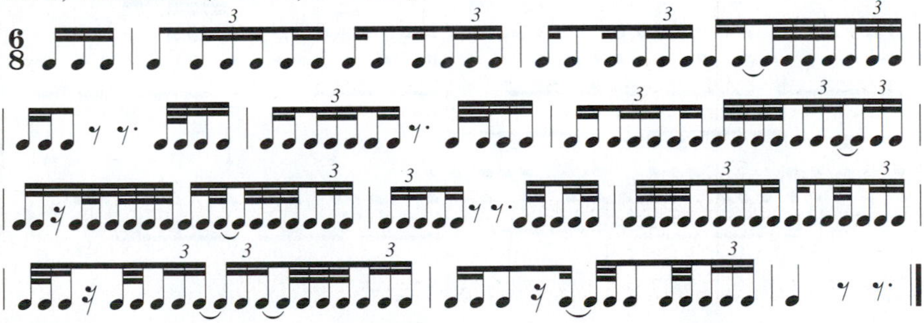

18. 4) ♩ = 40–52

18. G) Andante (♩ = 44)

18. H) Adagio (♪ = 92)

18. I) Largo ($\bullet$ = 44)

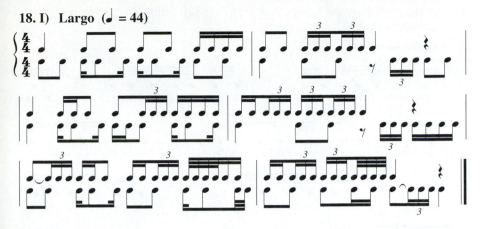

18. J) Adagio molto ($\bullet$ = 46)

18. K) Henry Wadsworth Longfellow (1807–1882), from "Walter von der Vogelweid" [1]

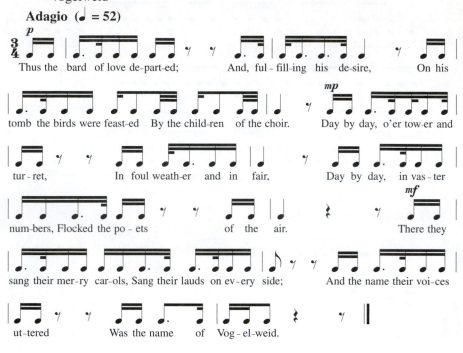

Adagio (♩ = 52)

Thus the bard of love de-part-ed; And, ful - fill-ing his de-sire, On his

tomb the birds were feast-ed By the child-ren of the choir. Day by day, o'er tow-er and

tur - ret, In foul weath-er and in fair, Day by day, in vas - ter

num-bers, Flocked the po - ets of the air. There they

sang their mer-ry car-ols, Sang their lauds on ev-ery side; And the name their voi-ces

ut-tered Was the name of Vog - el-weid.

NOTE

[1]German Minnesinger, ca. 1170–ca. 1230.

19. CHANGING SIMPLE METER

When changing meter, we must know what the new meter is well before beginning the measure. Even though it may seem difficult, conducting is particularly helpful in these studies because it forces us to be aware of the meter before we make the gesture of the downbeat, since that gesture is different in different meters. Good preparation for these studies is conducting the measures and simply counting the beats aloud, so we become familiar with the succession of meters before tackling the actual rhythms.

19. 1) ♩ = 100–176

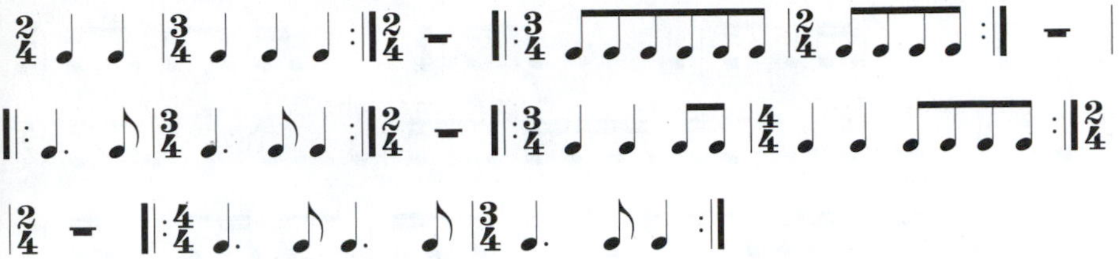

(rhythmic notation)

19. A) Vivace (♩ = 176)

(rhythmic notation)

19. B) Allegro (♩ = 160)

(rhythmic notation)

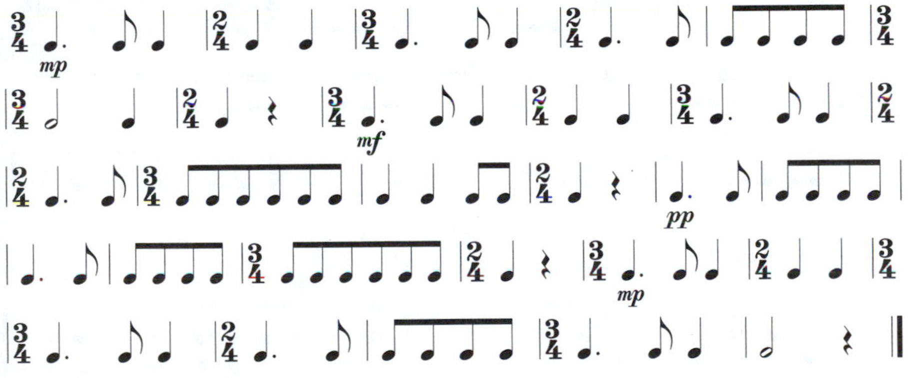

19. C) Presto (♩ = 192)

(rhythmic notation)

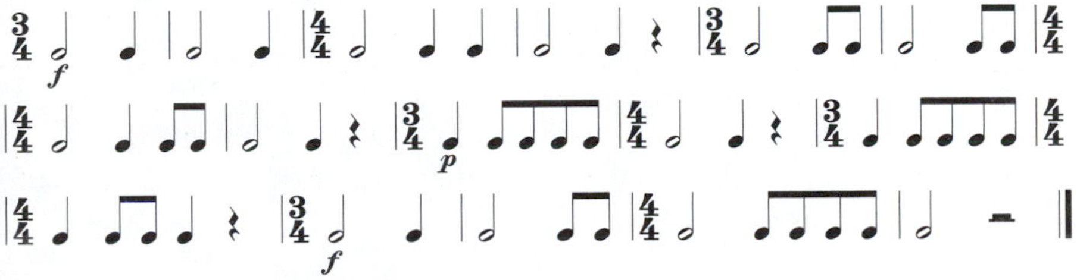

19. D) Allegretto (♩ = 80)

19. E) Allegro (♩ = 100)

19. 2) ♩ = 72–144

19. F) Allegro ($\downarrow$ = 132)

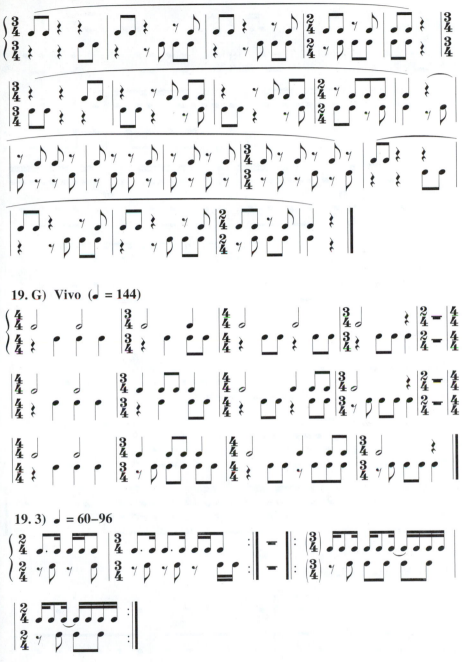

19. G) Vivo ($\downarrow$ = 144)

19. 3) $\downarrow$ = 60–96

19. H) Andante (♩ = 66)

19. I) Moderato (♩ = 72)

19. J) Vivo (♩ = 132)

19. K) Anne Bradstreet (1612–1672), from "Contemplations"

Andantino (♩ = 84)

mf

I heard the mer-ry grass-hop-per then sing, The black clad crick-et bear a sec-ond

part. They kept one tune and played on the same string, Seem-ing to glo-ry in their lit-tle

mp

art. Shall crea-tures ab-ject thus their voi-ces raise And in their kind re-sound their ma-ker's

pp

praise, Whilst I as mute, can war-ble forth no high-er lays?

20. CHANGING COMPOUND METER

As in changing simple meter, it is helpful to count the beats while conducting the meter before tackling the actual rhythm of each study. Conducting while performing the studies helps us feel physically the succession of meters.

20. 1) ♩. = 88–108

20. A) Vivo (♩. = 132)

20. B) Allegro (♩. = 92)

20. 2) ♩. = 56–76

20. C) Andante (♩. = 60)

20. D) Allegretto (♩. = 66)

20. 3) ♩. = 44–72

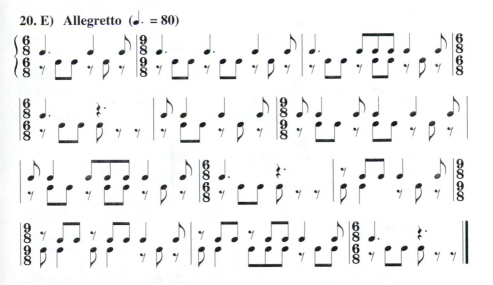

20. E) Allegretto (♩. = 80)

105

20. F) Andante (♩. = 52)

20. G) Andante (♩. = 54)

20. H) Andante (♩. = 69)

20. I) Stephen Crane (1871–1900), from *The Black Riders and Other Lines*

Allegretto (♩. = 80)

mp

Three lit-tle birds in a row sat mus-ing. A man passed near that place.

Then did the lit - tle birds nudge each o-ther. They said, "He thinks he can

mf

sing." They threw back their heads to laugh. With quaint coun-te-nan-ces they re-gard-ed

mp

him. They were ve - ry cu - ri-ous, those three lit-tle birds in a row.

21. CHANGING BETWEEN SIMPLE AND COMPOUND METER WITH THE DIVISION CONSTANT

When changing between simple and compound meter, as between two-four and six-eight time, there is normally an equivalence either between the beats or between the divisions of the beats. In this chapter, the division of the beat remains constant: when moving between two-four and six-eight, the eighth-note remains the same. This means that the beat is longer in compound meter, where it has three eighths instead of two, and so the tempo is slower. Moving from six-eight to two-four, the tempo speeds up because the beat is shorter. If the eighth-note is constant at 216, for example, the tempo in two-four or three-four will be half of that, ♩ = 108, while the tempo in six-eight or nine-eight will be a third of 216, or ♩. = 72. The tempi of the three note-values are given only for the first exercise and study; for the rest, those not given can be derived from those that are.

Tapping the eighth-note throughout a study, or using the metronome at the speed of the eighth, helps ensure the steadiness of the eighth as the meter changes. Counting the number of eighths on a beat, while conducting the meter, is a good preparation for the studies:

Normally, when meter changes between simple and compound, the equivalence ($\flat$ = $\flat$ or $\flat$. = $\flat$) must be shown at the point of the change. This has not been done in this chapter because the eighth is always constant.

21. 1) ♪ constant, ♩ = 72–120, ♩. = 48–80, ♪ = 144–240

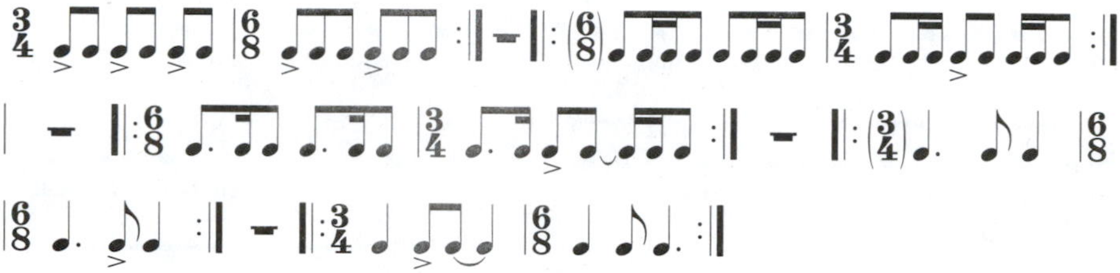

21. A) Andante, ♪ constant (♩. = 64, ♪ = 192, ♩ = 96)

21. B) Presto, ♪ constant (♩ = 144)

108

21. C) Allegretto, ♪ constant (♩. = 56)

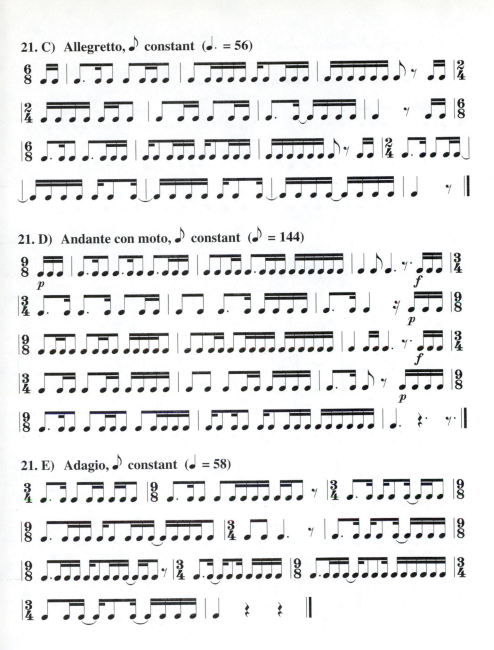

21. D) Andante con moto, ♪ constant (♩ = 144)

21. E) Adagio, ♪ constant (♩ = 58)

21. F) Allegro, ♪ constant (♩. = 72)

21. 2) ♪ constant, ♩. = 56–112

21. G) Presto, ♪ constant (♩. = 96)

21. H) Andante, ♪ constant (♩ = 63)

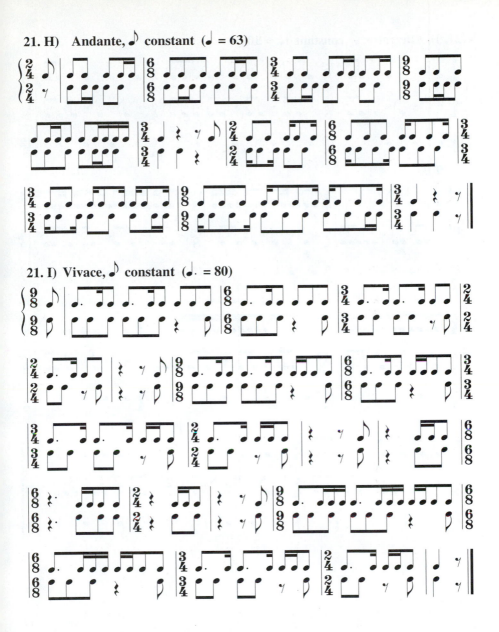

21. I) Vivace, ♪ constant (♩. = 80)

111

21. J) Allegretto, ♪ constant (♩ = 100)

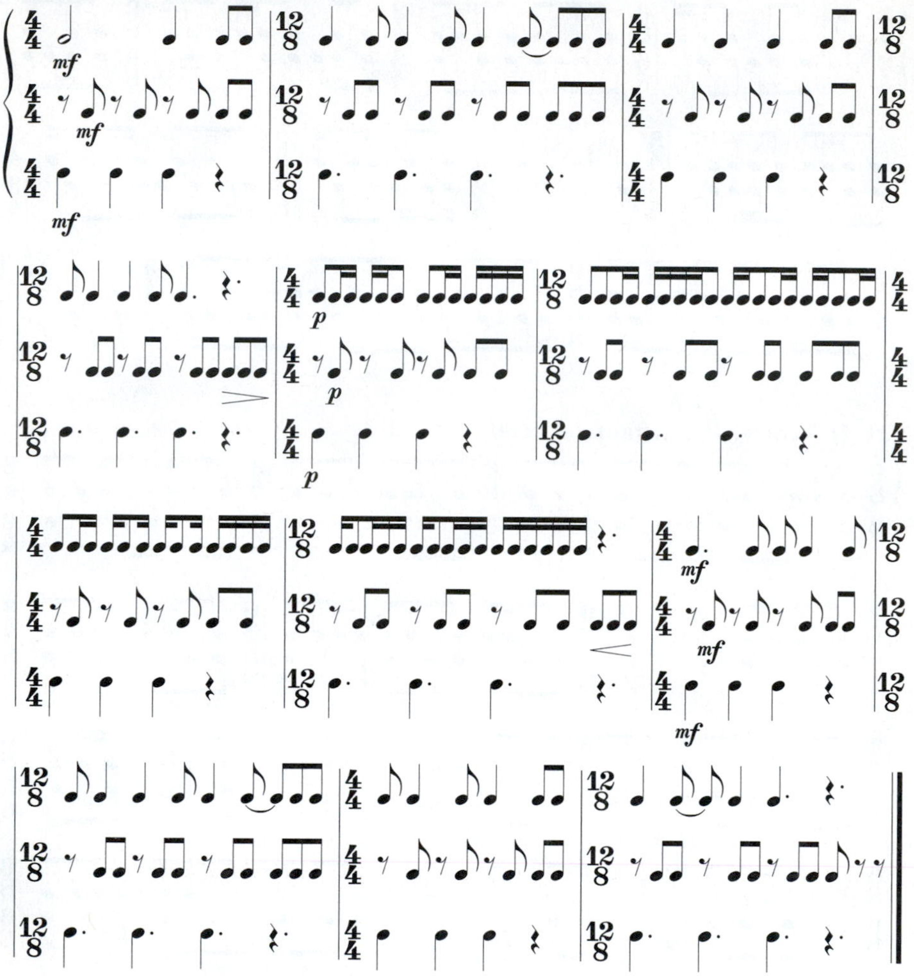

21. K) Langston Hughes (1902–1967), "Fantasy in Purple"[1]

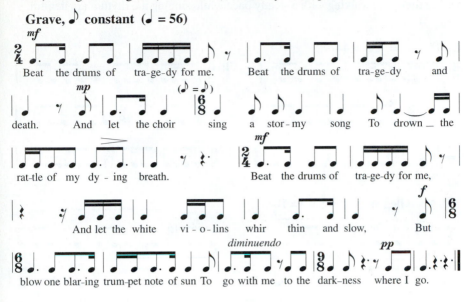

Grave, ♪ constant (♩ = 56)

Beat the drums of tra-ge-dy for me. Beat the drums of tra-ge-dy and

death. And let the choir sing a stor - my song To drown __ the

rat-tle of my dy - ing breath. Beat the drums of tra-ge-dy for me,

And let the white vi - o - lins whir thin and slow, But

blow one blar-ing trum-pet note of sun To go with me to the dark–ness where I go.

NOTE

[1]From COLLECTED POEMS by Langston Hughes. Copyright © 1994 by the Estate of Langston Hughes. Reprinted by permission of Alfred A. Knopf Inc.

22. CHANGING BETWEEN SIMPLE AND COMPOUND METER WITH THE BEAT CONSTANT

In this chapter the beat remains constant when the meter changes between simple and compound: the dotted quarter in compound meter equals the quarter-note in simple meter. Therefore, the speed of the eighth-note changes. The eighth-note in six-eight meter is only two-thirds as long as the eighth-note in two-four, for example. The change is the same as that between triplet and normal eighths in simple meter or between eighths and dotted eighths in compound meter. This is shown in Exercise 22.1, where the second segment, with change of meter, sounds the same as the first segment, where only the division of the beat changes; the same relation obtains between the third and fourth segments of this exercise.

When the beat remains constant, six-eight and two-four measures have the same length, as do three-four and nine-eight measures, because they have the same number of beats. In contrast, a six-eight measure, with two beats, will take less time than a three-four measure, even though the written note-values in the two measures may be identical, as in the first two measures of each phrase of Study 22.H.

The challenge here is to keep the beat constant. To this end, using a metronome, beating time, and walking with a steady pace while singing the rhythm are helpful.

22. 1) $\frac{6}{8}$ ♩. = $\frac{2}{4}$ ♩ = 44–72

22. A) Allegro, $\frac{6}{8}$ ♩. = $\frac{2}{4}$ ♩ (= 104)

22. B) Allegretto, $\frac{6}{8}$ ♩. = $\frac{2}{4}$ ♩ (= 72)

22. C) Andante, $\frac{9}{8}$ ♩. = $\frac{3}{4}$ ♩ (= 60)

22. D) Allegro ma non troppo, $\frac{6}{8}$ ♩. = $\frac{9}{8}$ ♩. = $\frac{3}{4}$ ♩ (= 92)

22. E) Allegretto, $\frac{9}{8}$ ♩. = $\frac{6}{8}$ ♩. = $\frac{3}{4}$ ♩ = $\frac{2}{4}$ ♩ (= 72)

22. 2) $\frac{6}{8}$ ♩. = $\frac{2}{4}$ ♩ = 52–72

22. F) Andante, $\frac{9}{8}$ ♩. = $\frac{3}{4}$ ♩ (= 58)

22. G) Adagio, $\frac{2}{4}$ ♩ = $\frac{6}{8}$ ♩. (= 52)

22. H) Allegretto, $\frac{3}{4}$ ♩ = $\frac{6}{8}$ ♩. (= 69)

22. I) Vivo $\frac{2}{4}$ ♩ = $\frac{6}{8}$ ♩. (= 112)

22. J) Thomas Dekker (1570?–1641?), "Golden Slumbers . . . "

23. THREE NOTES IN TWO BEATS; TWO NOTES IN THREE BEATS

The proportions involved in putting two equal notes in three beats and three equal notes in two beats are familiar from earlier chapters. In Chapter 10, two dotted eighths were put in a dotted-quarter beat; in Chapter 12, triplets were put in beats normally divided into two notes; in Chapter 13, two notes were put against three notes in a beat. What is new here is changing the division of the measure rather than the division of the beat.

In moving from normal quarter-notes to triplet quarters, it is helpful to think triplet eighths ahead of time, since two triplet eighths equal a triplet quarter: Thinking

facilitates performing = . Conducting helps steady the beat against which the cross-rhythms play. When we perform triplet quarter-notes, we must move quickly to the second note; when a triplet is performed unevenly, almost always it is the first note that is too long.

The hemiola pattern is most often three half-notes in the time of two three-four measures: . Study 23.F presents the hemiola rhythm in patterns familiar from the third movement of Schumann's Piano Concerto where, with one beat to a three-four measure, we hear the three half-notes against two downbeats.

23. 1) $\frac{6}{8}$ ♩. = $\frac{2}{4}$ ♩ = 63–108

23. A) Allegro moderato (♩. = 72)

23. B) Presto (♩ = 126)

23. C) Andante con moto (♩ = 80)

23. D) Allegro (♩ = 116)

23. E) Allegro moderato (♩ = 104)

23. 2) ♩. = 60–120 (Conduct one to a measure.)

23. H) Allegro (♩. = 100)

23. I)   Allegretto (♩. = 72)

23. J) Allegretto (♩ = 80)

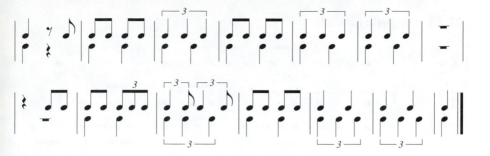

23. K) Allegro ($\quad$ = 120)

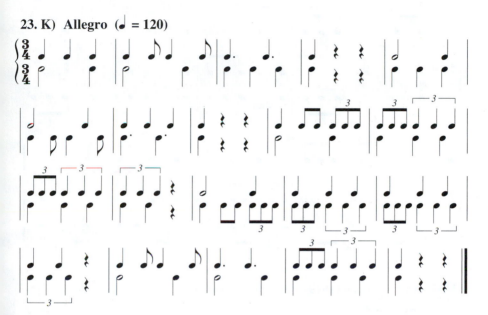

23. L) Allegretto (♩ = 80)

23. M) Walt Whitman (1819–1892), from *Leaves of Grass*

Allegro (♩ = 138)

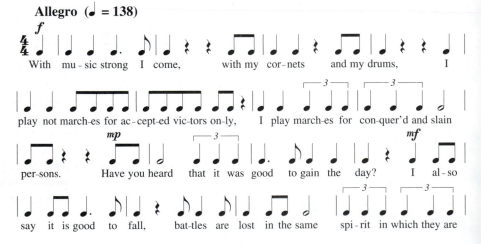

With mu - sic strong I come,   with my cor - nets   and my drums,   I

play not march-es for ac - cept-ed vic-tors on-ly,   I play march-es for con-quer'd and slain

per-sons.   Have you heard   that it was good   to gain the   day?   I   al - so

say   it is good   to   fall,   bat-tles are lost in the same   spi - rit in which they are

124

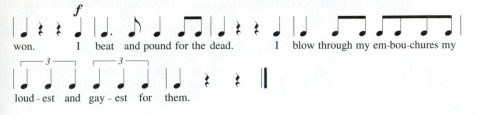

won.   I   beat and pound for the dead.   I   blow through my em-bou-chures my

loud-est and gay-est for them.

24. FOUR AGAINST THREE

As twelve is the common denominator of four and three, the rhythm of four six-teenth-notes against triplet eighths is measured in twelfths of a beat. The sixteenths are attacked on the first, fourth, seventh, and tenth parts of the beat, and the triplets are attacked on the first, fifth, and ninth parts of the beat. As with the performance of two against three, we may be aided by verbal phrases that we speak naturally in these rhythms:

Four against three:

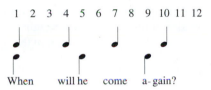

1 2 3 4 5 6 7 8 9 10 11 12

When   will he   come   a-gain?

To make a cross-rhythm of the four verbal accents sounding against three metrical accents, we write this as

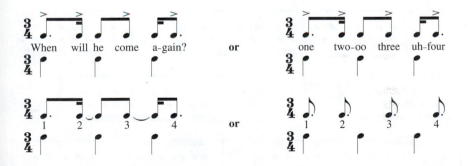

When will he come a-gain?   **or**   one   two-oo three uh-four

1   2   3   4   **or**   1   2   3   4

Similarly, three against four may be heard as

1 2 3 4 5 6 7 8 9 10 11 12

Wash   the car and wax it!

As a cross-rhythm of three accented syllables against four metrical accents, this is written

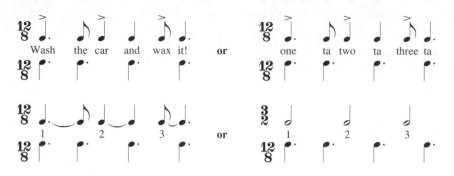

Wash the car and wax it! **or** one ta two ta three ta

1 2 3 **or** 1 2 3

The above patterns appear in Chapter 25 as a way of thinking four notes against three beats and vice versa, but practicing them quickly may help us learn to put four notes against three in a single beat.

It is important to practice the cross-rhythms slowly so as to ensure accuracy and quickly so as to arrive at the point where we hear not just the composite rhythm but each part independently. Finally, we should feel that we are performing two conflicting patterns at the same time and that, although they fit together correctly, neither one is based on the other. We don't think sixteenths and fit a triplet against them, or vice versa; we simply sing four sixteenths and clap three eighths, or sing a triplet and clap sixteenth notes, at the same time. We think two different thoughts simultaneously.

24. 1) ♩ = 40–72

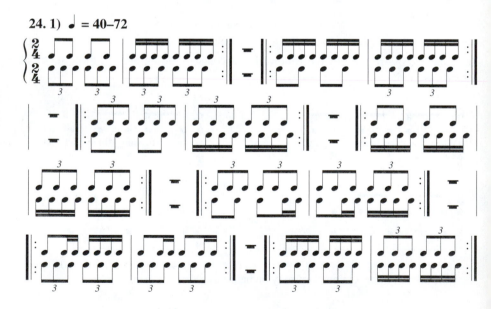

24. A) Andante ($\quarternote = 60$)

24. B) Allegretto ($\quarternote = 66$)

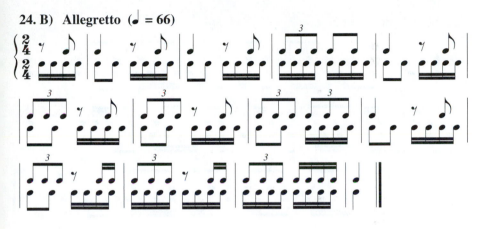

24. C) Andante ($\quarternote = 60$)

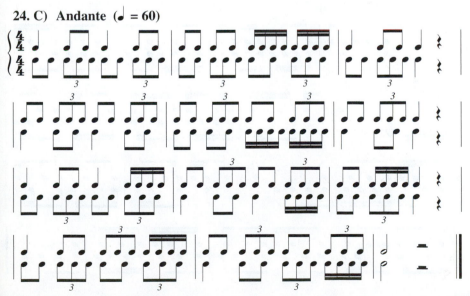

127

24. D) Allegretto $\frac{2}{4}$ ♩ = $\frac{6}{8}$ ♩. (= 72)

24. E) Adagio (♩ = 52)

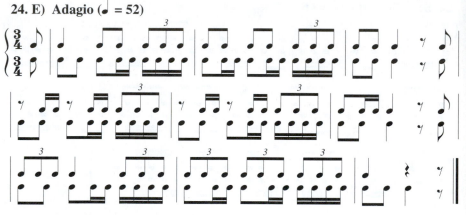

24. F) Adagio (♩ = 50)

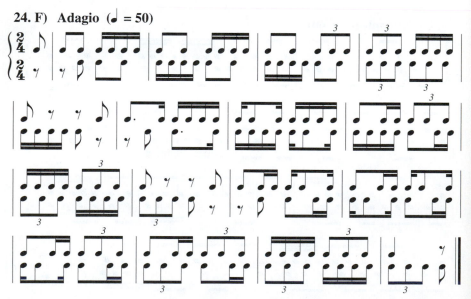

24. G) Andante (♩ = 72)

24. H) John Dryden (1631–1700) from "A Song for St. Cecilia's Day"

Allegro moderato (♩. = 69)

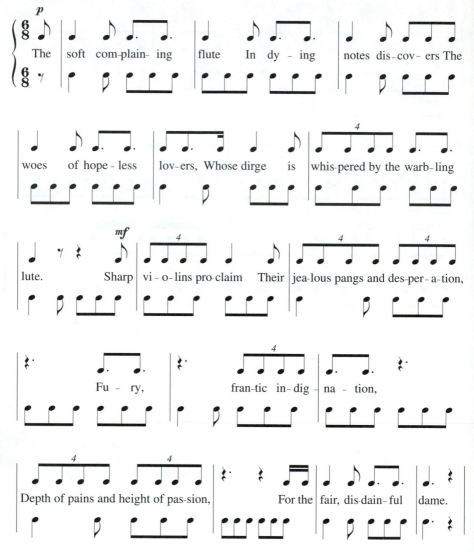

25. FOUR NOTES IN THREE BEATS; THREE NOTES IN FOUR BEATS

Singing four even notes in the time of three beats is performing four against three at the level of the measure. Each of the four quadruplet quarters in a three-four measure is three-quarters of a beat long; thus, the pattern can be notated as the equivalent of four dotted eighths, but it is more commonly notated as a quadruplet:

Singing three even notes in the time of four beats is most easily done in twelve-eight time, where each of the three notes has the value of four eighth-notes, or a half-note. When the meter is four-four, a background of triplet eighths should be imagined:

Tapping the note that is the common denominator (the sixteenth for four notes in three beats, the triplet eighth for three notes in four beats) will help us learn to hear the proportions correctly. As with other cross-rhythms, performance at a fast tempo is a process different from slow performance, so the patterns should be practiced both slowly and quickly.

25. 1) ♩ = 60–120 **(Measure 4 is equivalent to measure 3.)**

25. A) Adagio (♩ = 63)

25. B) Allegro (♩ = 120)

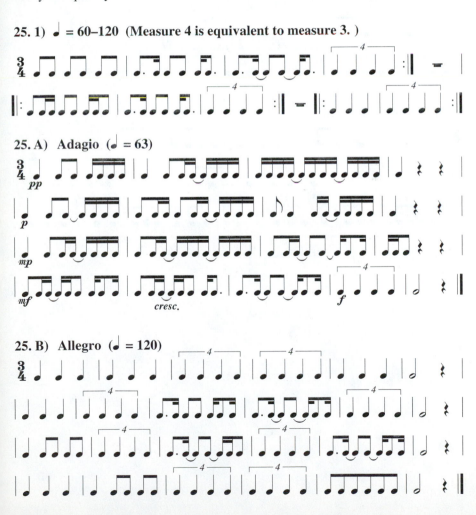

25. C) Moderato (♩ = 88)

25. 2) ¹²⁄₈ ♩. = ⁴⁄₄ ♩ = 60–132 (Measure 4 is equivalent to measure 3.)

25. D) Allegro (♩ = 126)

25. E) Allegretto (♩. = 112)

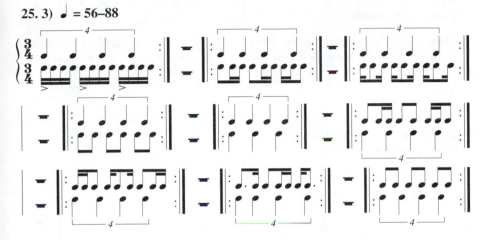

25. 3) ♩ = 56–88

25. F) Allegretto (♩ = 72)

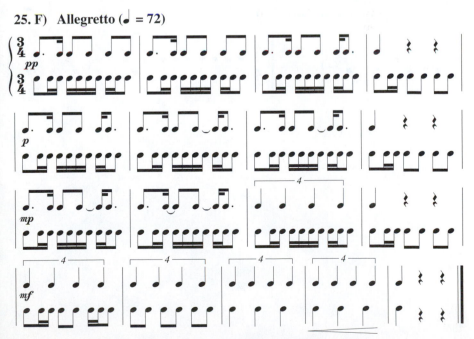

25. G) Con moto ($\quarternote$ = 80)

25. 4) $\frac{12}{8}$ $\dotted\quarternote$. = $\frac{4}{4}$ $\quarternote$ = 50–80

25. H) Allegretto (♩. = 96)

25. I) Allegretto (♩ = 100)

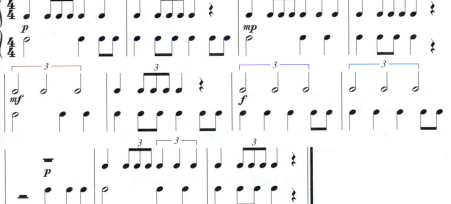

25. J) Allegretto (♩ = 88)

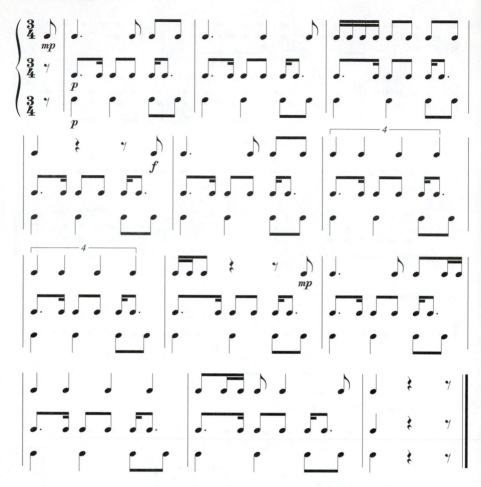

25. K) Anne Bradstreet (1612–1672), from "Mirth and Melancholy"

Andante (♩ = 80)

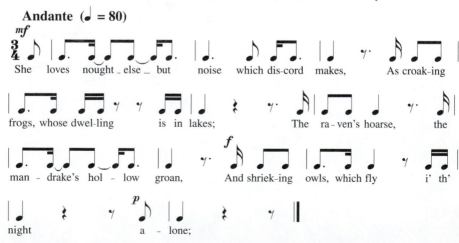

She loves nought else but noise which dis-cord makes, As croak-ing frogs, whose dwel-ling is in lakes; The ra-ven's hoarse, the man-drake's hol-low groan, And shriek-ing owls, which fly i' th' night a-lone;

26. QUINTUPLETS AND SEPTUPLETS

Counting the notes helps us put the five notes of a quintuplet onto a beat, especially in a context of other divisions of the beat:

To sing five equal notes in two beats, we need to think the quintuplet beat:

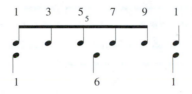

The common denominator of five and two is ten, but to perform five against two we need think only of the second note of the duplet dividing the third note of the quintuplet:

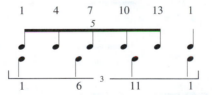

The common denominator of five and three is fifteen, so the second note of the triplet sounds a fifteenth of a beat before the third note of the quintuplet, and the third note of the triplet sounds a fifteenth of a beat after the fourth note of the quintuplet:

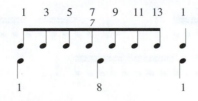

When an eighth-note quintuplet begins on the last quarter-note beat of a measure, its fourth note, which may look as if it falls on the following downbeat, actually sounds after the downbeat, as in the last phrase of Study 26.E.

Septuplets may be learned in the same way as quintuplets. When septuplet eighth-notes sound against two quarter-notes, the common denominator is fourteen, and the second quarter falls between the fourth and fifth notes of the septuplet:

As with all cross-rhythms, learning must begin with careful counting, proceed to slow performance where the subdivisions can be imagined and the composite rhythm heard to be accurate, and arrive at the stage where the patterns are performed and heard simultaneously and independently.

26. 1) ♩ = 48–76

26. A) Larghetto (♩ = 52)

26. B) Andante (♩ = 76)

26. 2) ♩ = 48–76

26. C) Andante (♩ = 63)

26. D) Allegro (♩ = 80)

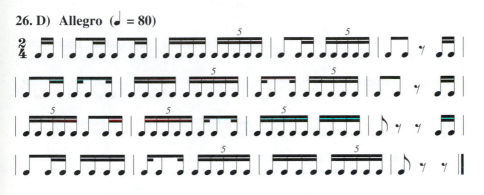

26. 3) ♩ = 54–80

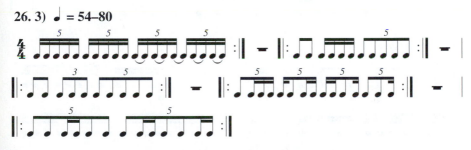

26. E) Allegretto (♩ = 76)

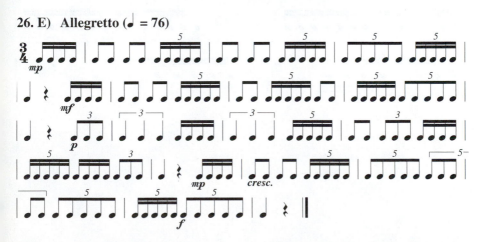

26. F) Andante (♩ = 60)

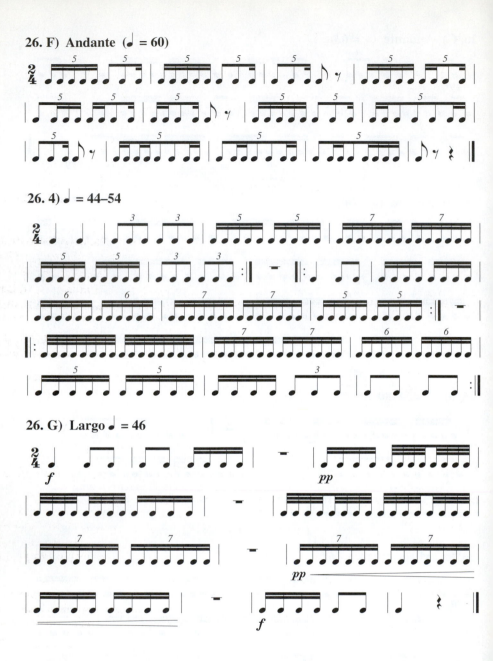

26. 4) ♩ = 44–54

26. G) Largo ♩ = 46

26. H) Largo molto (♩ = 40)

26. 5) ♩ = 40–69

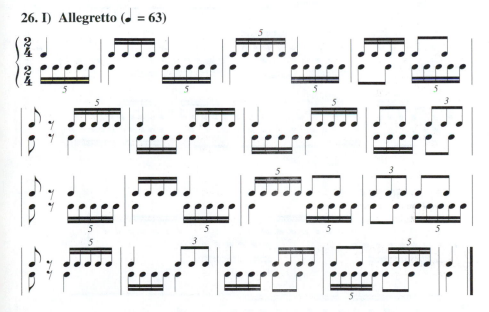

26. I) Allegretto (♩ = 63)

141

26. J) Moderato (♩ = 72)

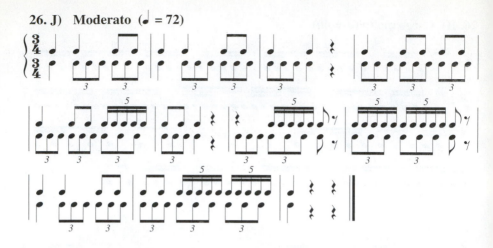

26. K) Andante (♩ = 60)

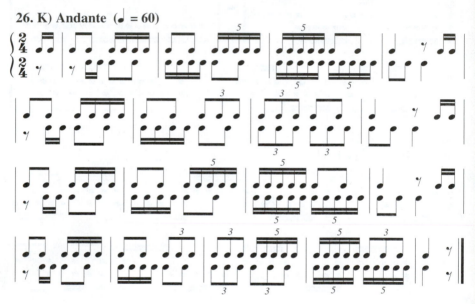

26. 6) ♩ = 40–54

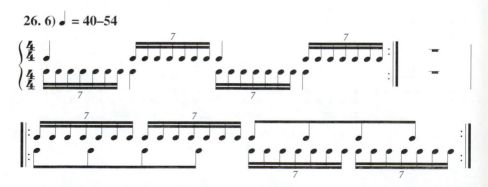

26. L) Adagio ($\quarternote = 40$)

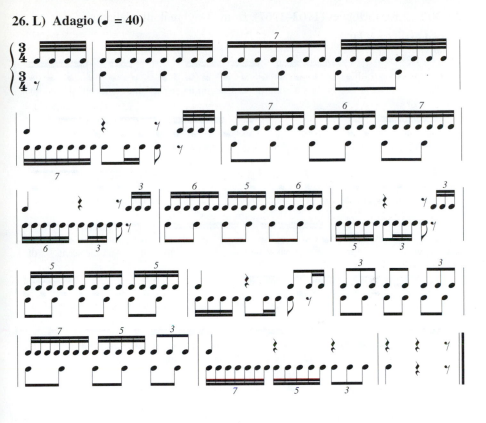

26. M) Andante ($\quarternote = 60$)

26. N) Langston Hughes (1902–1967), from "Daybreak in Alabama"[1]

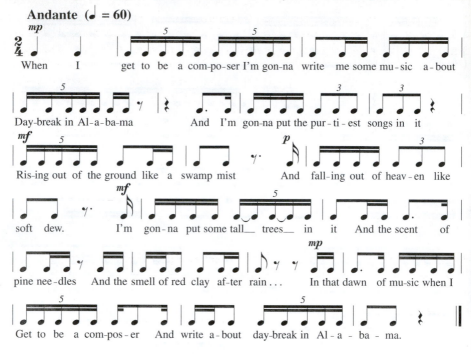

NOTE

[1]From COLLECTED POEMS by Langston Hughes. Copyright © 1994 by the Estate of Langston Hughes. Reprinted by permission of Alfred A. Knopf Inc.

27. FIVE-EIGHT METER

Five-eight measures may usually be understood as consisting of 2 + 3 or 3 + 2 eighths. Where the grouping is consistent, the meter signature will indicate it, as in the first two studies. Where the grouping is not consistent, as in the next three studies, beams will make the groups visible: ♩ ♪♪♪ is 3 + 2, whereas ♩ ♪♪♪ is 2 + 3. Because quarter-eighth is a more normal pattern than eighth-quarter, an eighth between two quarters may be assumed to belong to the first group—♩ ♪♩ is 3 + 2—when there is no contrary indication.

One standard pattern for conducting five beats is a modification of the pattern for conducting four, with an extra motion to the right (as in conducting six) before the upbeat when the pattern is 2 + 3, and an extra motion to the left when the pattern is 3 + 2. When approaching the rhythms in this chapter, it will be simpler to beat 3 followed by a smaller pattern for 2, or vice versa, depending on the structure of the measure.

While slow quintuple meter (as in Study 27.C) may be understood as having five beats in a measure, five-eight meter is most often not quintuple meter, but duple meter with two unequal beats, one a quarter-note and the other a dotted quarter. When the tempo of the eighth-note is 240 (as in Study 27.A), the quarter is 120 and the dotted quarter is 80, and these slower values are the effective tempo. Most of these studies should be understood, and conducted, not with five, but with two unequal beats in a measure. After striving to keep the beat steady, conducting unequal beats may seem strange, but we need to feel these beats physically. The other hand or a foot or metronome may mark the underlying quick pulse to keep the beats in their proper ratios.

27. 1) ♪ = 144–208

27. A) Allegro (in 2) (♪ = 240, ♩ = 120, ♩. = 80, ♩.⌣♩ = 48)

27. B) Vivace (♪ = 330)

27. C) Adagio ($\flat$ = 80)

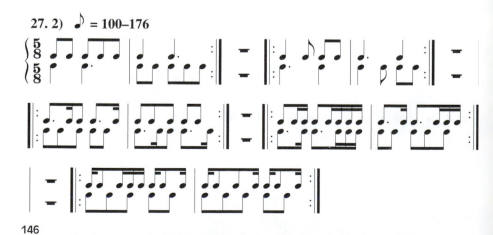

27. D) Allegro ($\flat$ = 192)

27. E) Andante ($\flat$ = 160)

27. 2) $\flat$ = 100–176

27. G) Andante ($\flat$ = 108)

27. H) Allegretto ($\flat$ = 132)

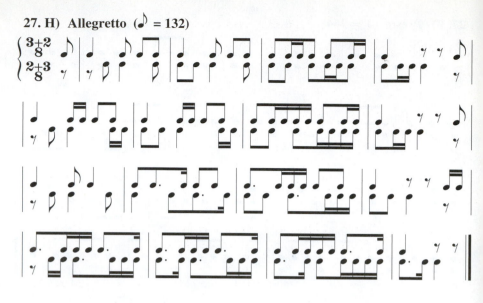

27. I) Vivace ($\flat$ = 208)

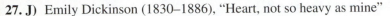

27. J) Emily Dickinson (1830–1886), "Heart, not so heavy as mine"

Andante ($\quarternote$ = 108)

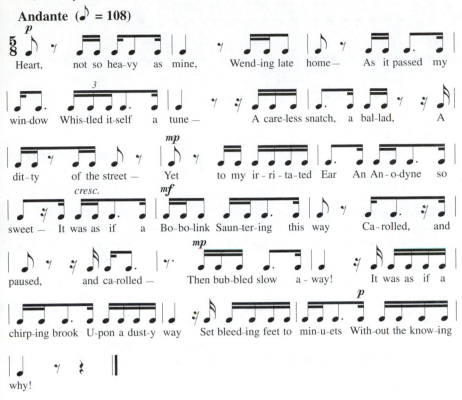

Heart, not so hea-vy as mine, Wend-ing late home— As it passed my

win-dow Whis-tled it-self a tune— A care-less snatch, a bal-lad, A

dit-ty of the street— Yet to my ir-ri-ta-ted Ear An An-o-dyne so

sweet— It was as if a Bo-bo-link Saun-ter-ing this way Ca-rolled, and

paused, and ca-rolled— Then bub-bled slow a-way! It was as if a

chirp-ing brook U-pon a dust-y way Set bleed-ing feet to min-u-ets With-out the know-ing

why!

28. MORE METERS WITH UNEQUAL BEATS

The meters in this chapter combine quarter-note and dotted-quarter beats just as five-eight meter does. Here, in each case, the meter signature makes the sequence of beats explicit. For example, $\frac{2+2+3}{8}$ is $\frac{7}{8}$, but with three beats of which the first two are quarters and the third is a dotted quarter. Conducting again helps us become comfortable with patterns of unequal beats, and tapping the underlying eighth-note helps us keep the proportions accurate.

28. 1) $\eighthnote$ = 160–288

28. A) Allegro ($\quarternote$ = 138, $\dottedquarter$ = 92)

$\frac{2+2+3}{8}$

28. 2) $\eighthnote$ = 160–208

$\frac{2+3+2}{8}$

28. B) Allegretto ($\eighthnote$ = 192)

$\frac{2+3+2}{8}$

28. 3) $\eighthnote$ = 160–208

$\frac{3+3+2}{8}$

28. C) Allegro ($\eighthnote$ = 208)

$\frac{3+3+2}{8}$

28. 4) ♪ = 160–224

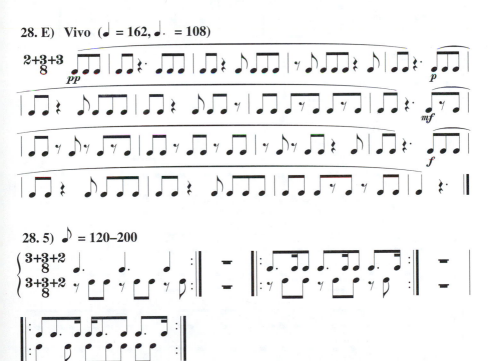

28. D) Andante con moto, in 4 (♪ = 160)

28. E) Vivo (♩ = 162, ♩. = 108)

28. 5) ♪ = 120–200

28. F) Allegretto (♪ = 184)

28. 6) ♪ = 144–224

28. G) Allegro (♪ = 216)

28. J) Samuel Taylor Coleridge (1772–1834), from *Rime of the Ancient Mariner*

Allegro (♩. = 80, ♩ = 120)

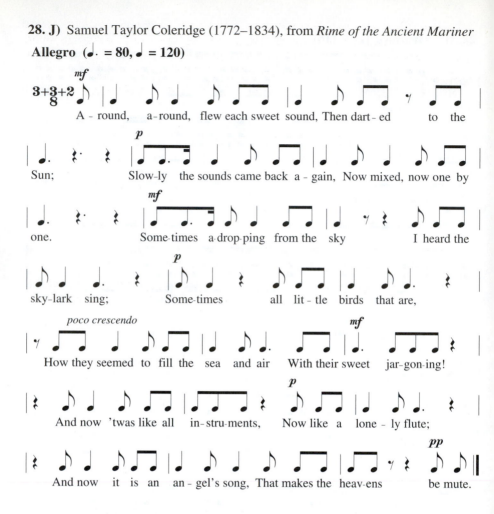

A - round, a - round, flew each sweet sound, Then dart - ed to the Sun; Slow-ly the sounds came back a - gain, Now mixed, now one by one. Some-times a-drop-ping from the sky I heard the sky-lark sing; Some-times all lit - tle birds that are, How they seemed to fill the sea and air With their sweet jar-gon-ing! And now 'twas like all in - stru-ments, Now like a lone - ly flute; And now it is an an - gel's song, That makes the heav-ens be mute.

29. CHANGING METERS WITH UNEQUAL BEATS

The best preparation for these studies is counting the eighths on each beat aloud while conducting the larger beats, thereby becoming familiar with the metrical patterns before attempting the actual rhythms. Thus, while conducting seven-eight in three and five-eight in two, we would count:

Tapping the eighth while singing the rhythm is especially important for studies such as 29.C where there are many notes and rests longer than eighths.

Studies 29.E and 29.G, and the exercises that immediately precede them, include three-sixteen and five-sixteen measures. The sixteenth-note rather than the eighth-note is the basic division of the beat, and beats are eighths and dotted eighths. In these studies, therefore, two-eight and five-sixteen measures have two beats, three-eight and seven-sixteen measures have three beats, and a three-sixteen measure is a single dotted-eighth beat.

29. 1) ♪ = 176–240

29. A) Allegretto, ♪ **constant** (♪ = 176)

29. B) Allegro (♪ = 208)

155

29. C) Vivace (♩. = 96, ♩ = 144)

29. D) Allegro (♩. = 72, ♩ = 108)

29. 2) ♪ constant, ♪ = 176–300

29. E) Presto, ♪ constant (♪ = 144)

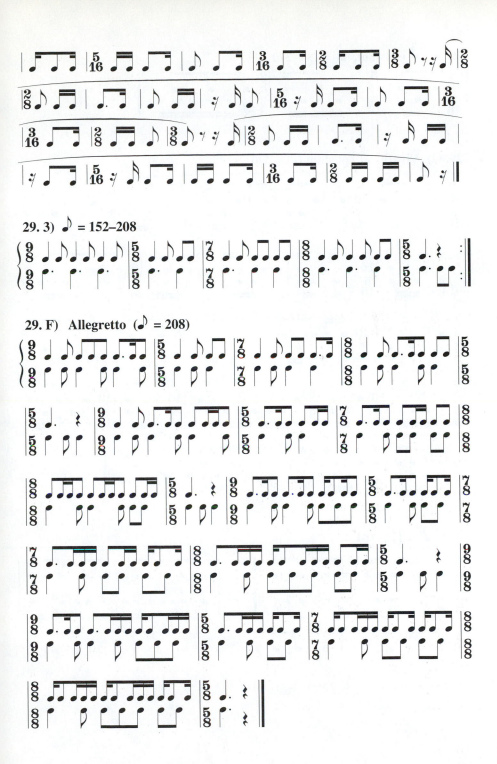

29. 3) ♪ = 152–208

29. F)   Allegretto (♩ = 208)

29. 4) ♪ constant, ♪ = 184–240

29. G) Vivace, ♪ constant (♪ = 240)

29. 5) ♪ = 120–184

29. H) Grazioso (♪ = 160)

29. I) Presto (♪ = 200)

29. J) Elizabeth Barrett Browning (1806–1861), from *Sonnets from the Portuguese*

Allegretto (♪ = 208)

Quick-lov-ing hearts, I thought, may quick-ly loathe; And, look-ing on my-self, I

seemed not one For such man's love! more like an out-of-tune Worn

viol, a good sing-er would be wroth To spoil his song with, and

which, snatched in haste, Is laid down at the first ill-sound-ing note.

30. MORE CROSS-RHYTHMS

The studies in this chapter are based on rhythmic patterns, combinations of rhythmic patterns, and the principle of ostinato found in music of West Africa.[1] In addition to the conflicting divisions of the beat (2 against 3 and 3 against 4) already studied, these rhythms involve different divisions of the measure in the two parts. The division of 6 into 2 groups of 3 and 3 groups of 2 (Studies 30.A and 30.B) is familiar from Chapter 23. New here is the grouping of twelve equal divisions of a measure into 5 plus 7, or 7 plus 5, against the normal 6 plus 6 or 4 groups of 3 or 3 groups of 4. Two studies (30.F and 30.G) involve cross-meters in ways that our conventional notation obscures, because, in order to show the equivalence of note-values in the two parts, one of them is notated with a ♩. ♩. ♩ pattern. The notation is that of compound meter, but we hear the pattern in simple meter.

As with all cross-rhythms, we first focus on the way the two parts fit together and then proceed to perform the two parts independently at the same time.

NOTE

[1] See, for example, John Miller Chernoff, *African Rhythm and African Sensibility* (Chicago and London: University of Chicago Press, 1979); A. M. Jones, *Studies in African Music* (London: Oxford University Press, 1959); and J. H. Kwabena Nketia, *African Music in Ghana* (Evanston: Northwestern University Press, 1963).

30. 1) ♩. = 56–92

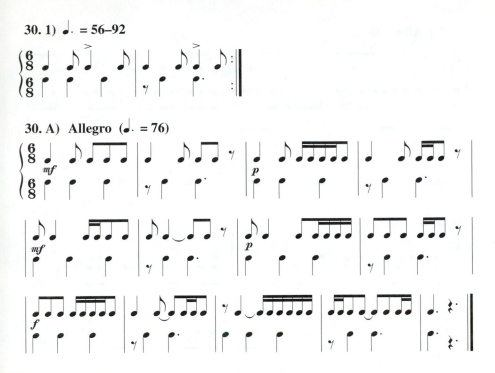

30. A) Allegro (♩. = 76)

30. 2) ♩. = 56–92

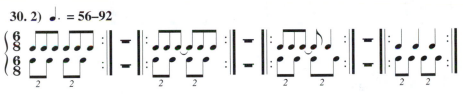

30. B) Allegro (♩. = 88)

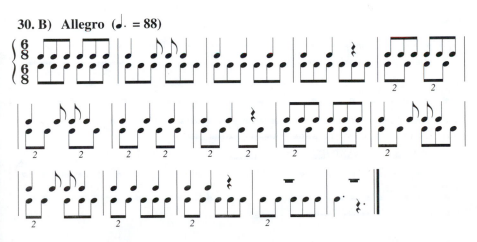

30. 3) ♩. = 40–60

30. C) Allegretto (♩. = 52)

30. 4) ♩. = 50–96

30. D) Allegro (♩. = 92)

30. 5) ♩ = 44–80

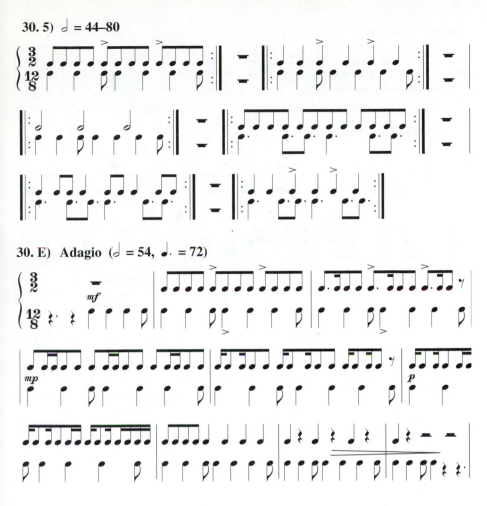

30. E) Adagio (♩ = 54, ♪. = 72)

30. F) Allegro (♩ = 72, ♪. = 96)

30. 6) ♩ = 50–100

30. G) Moderato (♩ = 96)

30. H) Allegro (♩ = 144, 𝅗𝅥 = 72, ♩. = 96)

30. I) Arthur William Edgar O'Shaughnessy (1844–1881), from "Ode"

Allegro ($\sphericalangle$ = 144, $\sphericalangle$. = 96)

f

We   are   the mu – sic – mak-ers, And | we are   the dream-ers   of dreams,

Wan – der-ing by lone   sea – break-ers, and | sit – ting   by de – so – late streams;

mp

World – los-ers and world – for-sak-ers, | On whom the pale moon gleams: Yet

f

p

we are the mov-ers   and | shak-ers Of the world for-ev-er,   it seems.

31. TEMPO MODULATION

In these studies, tempo is changed in two different ways. The same note-value may have the same speed in meters with different numbers of that value on the beat, so the beat becomes longer or shorter. For example, as we saw in Chapter 21, when the eighth-note stays the same in moving from simple to compound meter, the beat becomes longer and the tempo slower. Alternatively, different note-values may be given the same speed. For example, when a quintuplet sixteenth is equated to a preceding normal sixteenth, the beat, now consisting of five sixteenths, becomes longer. The terms *metric modulation* and *tempo modulation* have both been applied to these procedures for changing tempo, but the latter is more accurate.

Each of the preparatory exercises in this chapter should be performed three times in succession, beginning at the first of the indicated tempi; we will arrive at the other tempi during the course of the exercise. In the first exercise, 31.1a, if the quarter-note is initially 162, the eighth is 324, and the dotted quarter is 108; at the return to two-four, the 108 beat is kept; beginning again at 108, the eighth is 216, and the dotted quarter is 72; the third time we begin at 72, the eighth is 144, and the dotted quarter is 48, which is the speed of the final quarter-note.

It will be helpful to figure out the tempo at each point during the exercises and studies where values are marked as equivalent. As always, conducting will make us physically aware of the changes of tempo.

31. 1a) ♩ = 162, 108, 72, 48

31. 1b) ♩. = 48, 72, 108; ♩ = 72, 108, 162

31. 1c) ♩. = 48, 72, 108, 162

31. A) Beginning Vivace (♩ = 144, 96, 64)

31. B) Beginning Andante (beat = 48, 72, 108)

31. 2a) ♩ = 54, 72, 96, 128

31. 2b) ♩ = 128, 96, 72, 54

31. C) Beginning Andante (beat = 63, 84, 112, 84, 63)

31. D) Beginning Allegro (♩ = 128, 96, 72, 96, 128)

31. 3a) ♩ = **48, 60, 75**, *ca.* **94**

31. 3b) ♩ = **100, 80, 64**, *ca.* **51**

31. E) Beginning Moderato (♩ = **64, 80, 100, 80, 64**)

31. F) Beginning Lento (♩. = **40, 60, 90**)

31. G)   Beginning Adagio (beat = 50, 60, 72)

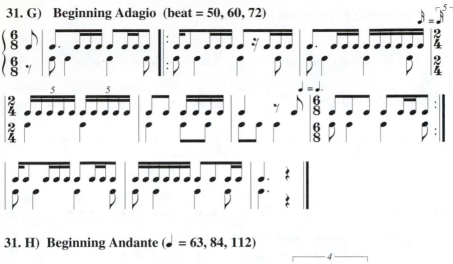

31. H)   Beginning Andante (♩ = 63, 84, 112)

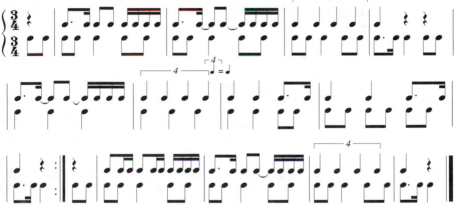

31. I) Beginning Presto (beat = 144, 96, 64)

31. J) Lewis Carroll (1832–1898), from *Alice in Wonderland*

Beginning Allegro (♩ = 108, 72, 48)